GETTING FROM HERE TO THERE

HOW SUCCESSFUL COMPANIES MANAGE SCALE

ASHISH BASU

INDIA · SINGAPORE · MALAYSIA

Notion Press

No.8, 3rd Cross Street
CIT Colony, Mylapore
Chennai, Tamil Nadu – 600004

First Published by Notion Press 2021
Copyright © Ashish Basu 2021
All Rights Reserved.

ISBN 978-1-63832-605-2

This book has been published with all efforts taken to make the material error-free after the consent of the author. However, the author and the publisher do not assume and hereby disclaim any liability to any party for any loss, damage, or disruption caused by errors or omissions, whether such errors or omissions result from negligence, accident, or any other cause.

While every effort has been made to avoid any mistake or omission, this publication is being sold on the condition and understanding that neither the author nor the publishers or printers would be liable in any manner to any person by reason of any mistake or omission in this publication or for any action taken or omitted to be taken or advice rendered or accepted on the basis of this work. For any defect in printing or binding the publishers will be liable only to replace the defective copy by another copy of this work then available.

Contents

Preface   5

The Genesis of Livewell   11

Section 1
Strategic Direction: Where Are You Going?

Prologue: Where Are You Going?   21

Mission: What's Your Core Purpose?   23

Vision: The Big Energizing Goal   30

Core Strategy: How You Will Win   36

Where Are You Going? Epilogue   56

Section 2
Breakthrough Initiatives: Getting the Big Things Right

Prologue: Getting the Big Things Right   67

Setting the Right Objectives   70

Strategic Programs for Your Objectives   77

Making Choices: The Strategy Matrix   83

Getting the Big Things Right: Epilogue   89

Section 3
The Management Process: Aligning the Organization

Prologue: Aligning the Organization	95
Measurement	101
Setting Goals across the Organization	113
Reviews and Reporting Systems	121
Aligning the Organization: Epilogue	134

Section 4
Building your Culture

Prologue: Building Your Culture	141
Building a Work Culture: Values and Policies	145
Building Organization Competence	153
Employee Morale and Belongingness	160
Building Your Culture: Epilogue	169
Annexure 1 Strategy Management Tools	*177*
Annexure 2 Evaluate Your Readiness To Scale	*187*

Preface

My first job was with NIIT, a global IT services company and a pioneer of computer education in India. NIIT had training centres in three cities at the time. I joined as a fresh MBA graduate having no real idea about what to expect or what I would do, but the belief that I would excel at it. I started out as a faculty member, teaching computers, while also being involved in software development projects.

Four years into my employment, NIIT decided to design and create their own training materials. Their goal was to increase learning effectiveness by providing students with more hands-on experience on computers. This was a novel idea at the time. In fact, I had completed several programming courses while doing my MBA without ever touching a computer. Since computers were still expensive, the idea was for students to write programs at home but then enter and debug the programs on actual computers at the centres.

This was my first experience in building a product. We assembled a team with members from across the company and started the work. There were very few computers available, so we would write the course material by hand, edit it, and then give it to an operator to type it in. We were the designers, curriculum managers, authors, spell-checkers, and editors. We were also the trainers, as we trained our faculty to deliver this product to students.

We launched the product nine months after we started. The company was fully committed to it. The centres had been changed to accommodate the new approach, so there was no going back. As it turned out, the student material had several errors. Some errors were minor, but others significantly impacted student learning. A combination of being a small company and having outstanding faculty saved NIIT from a major crisis.

Two years after that first experiment, I was asked to set up the Instructional R&D group. Since the discipline did not exist as a field of study in India at the time, there was no way to hire trained instructional designers. Instead, we hired writers and had a professor from the University of Michigan, Dr Glenn Knudsvig, come and teach us over several years. Our processes and competencies improved, and the team grew to build many successful programs.

We learned well enough to start an industry. Five years after the first program, we started to develop learning content for some of the world's leading companies. Today, a large percentage of the world's learning content is developed in India, and the origins of many leaders in content development can be traced to NIIT. The lesson I learned was that approaches that work at the start, do not work as you move further along.

Another key element was culture. NIIT still has a strong company culture, initially developed assiduously by Rajendra Pawar and Vijay Thadani. Its Mission Statement survives to this day, as does its values. We lived these values, though some were hard. We returned money to customers if they felt we did not deliver. As a pioneer, we knew we would make a few mistakes along the way, and our values recognized this as well.

NIITs culture was supported by a whole set of policies and rituals that engaged not just each employee but their families as well. During our annual day event, the chairman, CEO, and a few top executives would do everything—from planning the event to writing the speeches, finding the venues, ushering in the employees at the event, and organizing refreshments. This was our way of communicating that every employee was important. It also humanized top executives. There was an annual family day that was more like a picnic with families. We had a dating allowance, and we sent cakes to employees' grandmothers on their birthday.

Even though we took the culture for granted, it was a strong binding force in the company. As the company grew to have thousands of employees and a large extended network, employees poured their heart and soul into achieving goals that few companies could match in the 1990s. Even today, Forever NIITians (those who leave the company) have a special place in their heart for NIIT and extend their support wherever possible.

NIIT played a big role in building technology skills in India, and the relevance of technology has increased significantly in the past few decades. In the year 2000, only Microsoft made the list of the top five most valued companies. By 2020, there were no non-tech companies in the top five. Further, all five are platform companies, which means that their growth has changed the way customers and suppliers interact today. Google, Apple, Facebook and Amazon have shaped our lives in ways that were inconceivable two decades ago.

It is currently a great time for entrepreneurs. They can take advantage of networks to get to market quickly and to effectively outsource tasks that would take years to set up. They can disrupt the market using technology to improve a product or customer experience. The downside is that within a few years, another company can in turn disrupt their business with an innovation. The pace of technology advancement is so rapid that newer opportunities will continually be available.

In this book, I have assumed that your business is scalable, your market is large enough and growing, your company has adequate capital, your customers like your product, and you have access to the best ways to produce and deliver your product or service. This book shows you how to scale a business that is scalable.

> *This book shows you how to scale a business that is scalable.*

In the past thirty odd years, I have had the good fortune to have worn many hats and have worked with many outstanding large businesses and young start-ups. In a few cases, the focus was on increasing profitability or conserving cash. But in most cases, my focus has been to help scale the company. Whatever the challenge, there have been four levers to bring about the needed change.

This book is divided into four sections, each addressing one of the levers.

- Lever 1. Strategic Direction: The first section deals with the big picture, the purpose, the long-term goal, and Core Strategy. These are elements that are relatively unchanging and that serve to keep the company focused.
- Lever 2. Breakthrough Initiatives: The second section deals with selecting company-level priorities, the Breakthrough Objectives and programs that will take the company forward in the near term. We will discuss Strategy Matrix, a tool that represents the company's main priorities on one page, so that shifts required due to market changes can be taken quickly, but without derailing other important initiatives.
- Lever 3. The Management Process: The third section uses measurement, the Balanced Scorecard (BSC) and Objectives and Key Results (OKRs) to institute a transparent and participatory management system that allows employees to align themselves to changing company priorities.
- Lever 4. Culture and Competency: The fourth section is about instituting a culture within the organization using shared values, and an approach to continuously enhance skills within the company, so that employees want to grow the company and have the competencies to do it.

In each section, we follow the story of Ankit and Subodh and their company Livewell as they explore the situations faced by many leaders. The company is fictional, but each of their challenges are taken from real companies. Within their story are chapters explaining concepts and tools that you can use to build your organization.

The ideas behind the four levers are valid for all sizes of organizations: from start-ups with less than twenty employees to large organizations with more than ten thousand.

There are two annexures that can help you quickly implement some of the ideas in the book.

1. Strategy Management Tools: This is a list and a short description of management tools that are helpful in thinking through and defining your strategy.
2. Evaluate Your Readiness to Scale: A simple questionnaire that helps you rate each of the levers in your organization and help prioritize your attention.

Many people have indirectly contributed to this book by providing the environment and opportunities to develop these ideas.

To Rajendra Pawar and Vijay Thadani, co-founders of NIIT, who have guided me throughout my career and continue to remain well-wishers and mentors till today. They provided me the opportunity to experiment and learn. Many of the anecdotes and experiences mentioned in this book would not have been possible without their support.

To Cyrus Guzder of AFL, Sanjay Kapoor – earlier CEO Airtel, Pramod Bhasin – founder Genpact, for being exemplars of leadership and management that helped me understand how different styles of leadership could be successful and why all the four levers were important.

To Pradeep Singh, Will Poole, Geeta Goel, and Vivek Agarwal, who provided me with opportunities to put the levers to practice.

To all my colleagues and friends in the organizations that I have been associated with either as an employee or a consultant. I would need another book to name you all and how you helped me in developing and validating the methods that worked and those that did not.

Others have contributed directly to this book.

Preface

To my batch and extended family from IIM Bangalore. For thirty-five odd years, this group has continually provided encouragement without being judgemental. Specially, Debjani Biswas for talking me into writing the book during a bus ride from Patan Mahal to Delhi, and Shripad Nadkarni for telling me how not to name the book.

To Mani Subramani, Mohan Subramaniam, Gautam Brahma, Ravi Kittu, Vasant Naik, and Ciby James for painstakingly reviewing the book and providing detailed feedback. I have them to thank for delaying the book by over three months with their insightful comments that required extensive rework.

To my son Akash for reading this book which is not remotely in his areas of interest and providing his feedback. To my daughter Shreya for volunteering her time to keep this project on schedule and coordinate outreach activities. And finally, to my wife and partner Kalpana for her continuous support and encouragement through the entire process of writing, and for being a sounding board for the ideas and structure as it developed.

I hope you enjoy this book.

The Genesis of Livewell

Subodh was excited.

After many years of struggle, his fledgling company, Livewell.com, had successfully closed a sizable funding round. They finally had enough cash to implement some of his ideas.

Subodh grew up in a small town in Punjab in a family of traders. The youngest of five children, he was left largely to himself, and found that he liked it. He took to books at an early age and to maths soon after. His academic prowess was soon the talk of the village and later of the nearby town. After completing school, he took the competitive exam for admission to IIT and, to no one's surprise, did very well and chose to study Computer Science in Delhi.

IIT was a shock for Subodh. From being the brightest person in his school and the teacher's pet, he found himself struggling to keep up. To add to his misery, he did not like hostel food and started losing weight. He had always been healthy, but in his first term he missed nearly two weeks of classes due to illness.

From his second term onwards, he added personal health to his regular academic goals. He ate well, started to exercise, and monitored everything through apps. He met Ankit during an early morning jog, and strangely enough they became friends. It was strange because Ankit was the antithesis of Subodh in many ways. He grew up in Mumbai, was charming and outgoing, and was captain of the school cricket team with national honours in swimming. He could do anything he wanted, and he had joined IIT because he could, and because a friend dared him.

Fitness brought Subodh and Ankit together. Sometime in their third year, they decided to build a fitness app that was better than anything else in the market. They soon realized they needed sensors to build anything more than a basic app. They roped in Supriya, who was an electronics whiz. She put together a band with sensors that could track a whole range of body functions including motion, heartbeat, location, sweat, and blood pressure.

Their project was selected to represent IIT at a premier tech event, and they won. After returning from the competition, the three of them met to decide if they wanted to continue working on the app. Supriya did not see this as a major goal and wanted to pursue further studies in the United States. She was, however, prepared to help for a while. Ankit and Subodh wanted to see if they could take the app further.

They decided to extend the idea to more for than just fitness enthusiasts. Over their next two terms, they enhanced both the product and the idea. The band was now paired with an app that used all the collected information to provide advanced analytics. This information could be available to both the person with the band and to healthcare professionals. It was significantly more advanced than other similar health wearables. They decided to call their company and their product Livewell.

They joined an accelerator immediately after graduation, and within six months had active interest from several seed investors. They were one of the lucky few who were able to select the investors they wanted. They were able to hire a great team and build out their product. They moved into a nice co-working space with flexibility to grow as they wanted. It was a fairy-tale beginning.

The challenges started about six months into their first year, after they got their seed investment. Supriya felt the main challenge was over and she left to pursue her master's degree. The initial prototype was bulky, and they worked with a Chinese IoT manufacturer to improve their device. The first lot looked great, but the sensors did not work as expected. Ankit moved to China for two months to find a better manufacturer. They had hoped to release the product within a year of funding. It took another six months till they finally got it out.

By then, they had run out of money. They had to move out of their office and into an apartment, and they had let go most of their team. They borrowed money from friends to pay salaries. Fortunately, one of their investors provided additional funding to get the first batch of a thousand pieces developed and delivered. Since they had no money for marketing, Subodh started meeting doctors with the device and the data. After what seemed like a million trials, one of the doctors, Dr Kamini Bhat, was excited enough to recommend Livewell to her patients.

Subodh and Ankit were now both meeting investors and trying to raise the next round of funding. Since the product had very few active customers, this turned out to be a nightmare. While in their earlier round, seed investors were lining up to invest, now there was simply no interest.

And then a miracle happened. One of Kamini's patients was a senior partner in a VC firm. He loved the product, and invited Subodh and Ankit over for dinner. Within a month, they had been approved for enough cash infusion to get them going. There were of course many conditions, and it was a significant dilution of equity. But the sun was shining again. They set up a new office and were lucky to get back some of the people who had left.

They hired a marketing team as well. Their social media presence started to grow, and a few stores started to carry their product. They put it on all the major marketplaces as well. Their newly hired technology team had significantly improved the look and functionality of the product. Their manufacturing was now reliable. Their new investor helped them file a slew of patents to make their approach defensible. Their board was expanded to include Kamini Bhat and a new investor nominee, Kriti Rao.

Sales started to rise. Device sales increased each quarter. They were now midway through their third year and were being talked about as one of the start-ups that could disrupt the wearable market. Subodh, Ankit, Kriti, and Kamini would meet every month to review what they had achieved and to plan for the next month.

During one of the meetings, the discussion turned to the future. "We know we are doing well right now," said Ankit, "but how do we ensure we stay ahead? There will always be something newer, and as technology continues to evolve, we need to be ahead of everyone else. What works today, may not work tomorrow."

"It's more than just that," said Subodh. "Today, we are doing a lot of the thinking for the business. But as we grow, and I am hoping we grow a lot more, our entire company needs to be ready to quickly adapt to changes. We have to expand our leadership team and share decision-making."

Kriti nodded. "It's great that you are thinking about this and wanting to reliably scale your business. As you start to scale, you need an organization that has clarity of purpose and can respond quickly when it needs to. I know a person, Javed Ali, who can help you put together some of the elements that will help."

Subodh looked uncertain. "I like the idea. But it seems like a lot of work to take on right now."

Kriti smiled. "I think you will find that it is best to have some of this set up as early as possible. As the company grows, it will become harder to make it flexible. It should also take some pressure off from the two of you. It will take some of your time to implement, but you do not need to do it all at once. If you are clear about what you want, you can decide when and how fast you want to do it."

"That makes sense," said Subodh. "We should meet Javed."

Both Subodh and Kamini nodded. Kriti agreed to connect Javed with Subodh and Ankit.

Subodh and Ankit invited Javed to meet them over the next week. Javed was an older man and seemed to have done everything. He had grown companies as a CEO, had acquired and integrated companies, done three start-ups, and was on the board of an impact fund. He had even started a fund himself.

He was quiet, unassuming, and asked a lot of questions. He took the time to understand their business and was able to give examples of other businesses similar to Livewell's. He explained his approach, and both Ankit and Subodh felt he would be the right person to help them. Ankit suggested that they invite Kriti and Kamini for their next meeting. Javed agreed and asked for information about the company to prepare better for the meeting.

After introducing Javed to Kamini, Subodh asked Javed to take over.

"It's clear that you want to be able to scale. Before I try and provide a way of looking at this, I would like to understand what you think is the most important attribute for scale," Javed said, "Can each of you write down your reason for wanting this?"

Kamini nodded. "How many attributes can I write? I can think of several."

"Just one," said Javed. "If you can think of several, pick the one most important to you."

After a few minutes, everyone had their reasons written down.

Kamini went first. "I think the key element is the culture of the organization. If every Livewell employee wants us to succeed, we will."

Subodh said, "My key attribute adds to Kamini's thought. I think we will be best able to scale if every employee can contribute their ideas and then execute them."

Ankit said, "I think we will be able to scale if at any time we focus on a few things and do them very well."

Everyone now looked towards Kriti, who hesitated. "My bigger problem is that I am not clear about where we are headed. Once we know that, it would be good to be clear about how we will get there."

Javed had been taking notes while the others were speaking. "This is wonderful. Between the four of you, you have very clearly articulated the key attributes required for scale." He went to the whiteboard and drew a diagram.

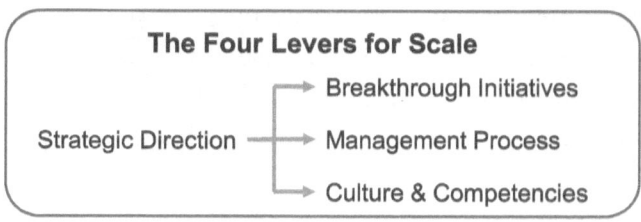

Javed continued, "Together you have identified all four levers for scaling Livewell. Put simply, these levers allow you to grow while adapting to the changing industry and customer requirements. These are the levers you control. What you do with the levers depends on your industry, competition, customer preferences and, most importantly, access to capital."

"This seems simple enough," said Kamini. "How does this address everything we mentioned?"

Javed smiled and looked at his notes. "Let's start with Kriti. She wanted to know where Livewell is headed and how to get there. That is our Strategic Direction. We will define our purpose and goal through our Vision and Mission. We will then outline our Core Strategy, which is the broad how of getting where we want to go.

Ankit wanted a few focus areas which could change easily. Those are Breakthrough Initiatives. We will identify objectives and programs to focus on and will represent them in a 'Strategy Matrix'.

Subodh asked for a transparent method to have everyone contribute ideas and execute them on a near-continuous basis. You can do that through setting up a company-wide Management Process.

Finally, Kamini spoke about a culture where people want to, and can, contribute to the company. Here we will set up our values as well as a process to build people competencies on an ongoing basis. We will use practices and policies to build trust, so that employees want to participate in our continued success."

"That became heavy very quickly," said Subodh. "I am guessing each of these will need a lot of work. Is there a sequence we should follow?"

"Not really. You should have clarity on your purpose and direction first, but the rest depends on what your challenges are at that time. These are organization-wide processes, and it will take some time and effort to implement all of them. It's a good idea to do them one at a time," said Javed.

Ankit nodded. "I like this framework and believe it will help us scale more effectively. If we can respond faster than our competitors, it will be a huge advantage. And if we can take everyone along, Livewell will become a wonderful place to work as well."

"I couldn't have put it better myself," said Javed. "Many things go into making your company a success. Your strategy, the industry, understanding the pulse of the customer, having the right people and the right technology—everything matters. Occasionally it is luck or timing, and often its money. The four levers help you use your resources most effectively to respond to market changes while doing what is required to grow."

Subodh said, "Well Javed, you have convinced us. Let's get started with the first part of your framework and take it from there. Ankit, you and I can have a more detailed session in our office, and perhaps meet again after two weeks?"

Everyone nodded.

SECTION 1
Strategic Direction: Where Are You Going?

One day Alice came to a fork in the road and saw a Chershire cat in a tree.

"Which road do I take?", she asked.

"Where do you want to go?", Was his response.

"I don't know", Alice answered.

"Then", said the cat, "it doesn't matter".

– Lewis Carroll,
Alice's Adventures in Wonderland

Prologue: Where Are You Going?

A week after their first meeting, Javed met Ankit and Subodh at the Livewell office and explained his process. He planned to facilitate the process, and not prescribe a solution. In order to do that, he would need to understand the company better so that he would know the context better and could share examples and experiences that were relevant.

Ankit and Subodh both felt this would be better than a more prescriptive approach.

Javed spent the next few days reviewing all the public information available about Livewell. He also asked Subodh to share Livewell's history, financial performance and plans. He met with the product and marketing teams to better understand the product, the industry and Livewell's customers. He completed all this in the two weeks prior to the next meeting of the core team.

Once they were all together, Javed outlined the first phase of the approach. "The last time we met, we talked about the four elements and that we would take up the first one today." He put up his earlier diagram

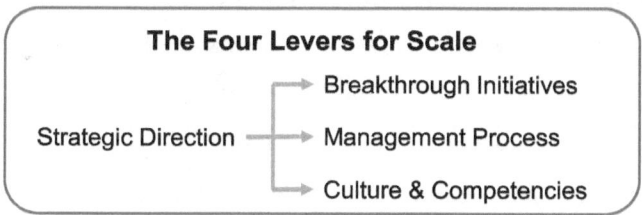

"As we had discussed earlier, we will start with our Strategic Direction. The idea is to define where we are going. This has three elements:

Lever 1. Strategic Direction

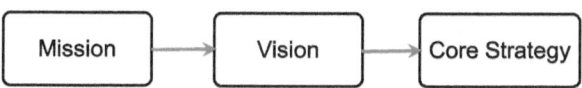

The first part is to understand why the company exists – its purpose. There are so many different things we could have done. Why Livewell? Every company needs a purpose to guide everything else. This is its Mission Statement.

The second is to set a Big Hairy Audacious Goal—one that can define our ambitions. This is the Vision Statement."

"Hold on a minute," Ankit interrupted. "I understand that perhaps our reason to exist will not change, but a big goal we set now may not be relevant in our future."

"Good point," said Javed. "Your Mission is likely to last a long time if you get it right. But your Vision is something which often has a date by when you want to reach it—it just may happen to be many years in your future. And your dreams may change. Then you should reset your Vision."

Ankit nodded.

"To continue, the third part we need to get to is your Core Strategy. This outlines the key elements that define your business and your competitive advantage. Here you will define your customer, the needs you will meet and how you will be distinctive in meeting your customer's needs. And again, this may also change over time."

"This is interesting," Kriti said. "We are setting up the Why, What and How for the company. The Mission seems like the 'why', the Vision is the 'what' and Core Strategies are the 'how'."

"Very good," Javed said. "I couldn't have put it better myself."

"Fair enough," said Ankit. "So, what are the next steps?"

"We will need to have one or two meetings between the five of us to put together the Vision and Mission, and then get a few more folks from your management team together to put together the Core Strategy."

"Right," said Ankit. "That sounds like a plan. Let's set a date for the first meeting, shall we?"

Mission: What's Your Core Purpose?

If you ask the question "Why does *a* company exist?" you will get many answers. A popular answer is that it exists to ensure returns to your shareholders. However, if the question is "Why does *your* company exist," you need to find that answer for yourself. The answer to that question is your Mission, your core purpose. The answer should be short, clear and unchanging. It should touch the heart more than it does the mind.

Let us look at a few examples. Disney's current Corporate Mission Statement is:

"To be one of the world's leading producers and providers of entertainment and information. Using our portfolio of brands to differentiate our content, services and consumer products, we seek to develop the most creative, innovative and profitable entertainment experiences and related products in the world."

Let us examine this Statement. It suggests building its brands, and it is very clearly in the entertainment business. It is all encompassing in that 'related products' can be anything. But it does not touch the heart; there is no feeling associated with the Statement.

Compare this with their original Mission, their core purpose: "to make people happy." That Mission was much more powerful. It was simple, comprising just four words. It is almost possible to see the kind of people who work in the company, feel the drive of Walt Disney and revel in their success. It has a feeling of joy that was communicated in all initial Disney endeavours. It is so powerful that this Mission Statement continues to guide the organization even when it is replaced. Using a human analogy, the Mission is the soul of the company.

The soul of a company does not need to be soft and mushy. Today, Nike's Mission is "to bring inspiration and innovation to every athlete in the world." Nike is certainly very innovative in its shoes. The Nike brand, with its famous swish logo and the exhortation to 'just do it', is powerful. But it has been sanitized to be more easily communicable to the outside world. Years ago, its Mission was "to experience the emotion of competition, winning and crushing competitors." It was raw, direct and clear about why it existed. In their early years, Nike was the upstart that took on the then leader, Adidas. Their direct focus on their competitor helped them get ahead.

NIIT, the pioneer of IT Education in India, had an initial Mission of "Bringing people and computers together, successfully." Through the 1980s and the 1990s, NIIT trained its students and provided the IT industry with the personnel it needed. Over time, it has branched out into corporate IT training, and it continues to bring people and computers together.

In the start-up culture in India today, the quality of focus is highly valued and is reflected in various companies' Mission Statements. Zomato's Mission is "to ensure no one has a bad meal." The company initially put pictures of restaurant menus on a website and allowed users to comment and share their experiences. Over time, they expanded their service, and they now deliver food and book seats at restaurants. User ranking remains a key feature of all their activities, and they are always available to support users if there is a problem with food delivery. They remain true to their Mission.

Why is a Mission Important?

In the book 'Built to Last', Jim Collins and his team compared visionary companies to their nearest competitors. One of the key differentiators they found between great and good companies was that great companies remained true to their 'core ideology'. This is their reason for existence, and their Mission.

Many companies start with a core ideology—often reflected in the passion of their founders. However, over time, this is often diluted or lost. As new managers join the organization, many of them do not have much access to the founders. These people view the company through their own lens and context, which may not be aligned to the ideology of the company.

> The Mission Statement outlines the company's core ideology, the reason (why) they exist

It is not only new employees who may not be aligned to the ideology. Founders themselves are often subject to many pressures and may find themselves taking some short-term decisions that may not be aligned to their initial purpose for setting up the company. Writing the Mission and revisiting it often gives the founders continuing clarity. And if this is shared with the investors at the start, the company will have investors who are also aligned to the company's Mission.

The Mission Statement is usually shared both within and outside your organization. The reason for sharing is a little different for each type of stakeholder.

1. Employees: Your employees are the most important group that must relate to your Mission. You can consider it a vaccination. Whenever a decision is taken that may subvert the Mission, the antibodies created by the vaccine should prevent such a decision. For example, if Zomato ranked restaurants based on how much revenue they generated for Zomato, they would diverge from their Mission: "To ensure no one has a bad meal."
2. Investors and Shareholders: People putting money into your company should know what they are getting into. The Mission clarifies your core ideology. This may not be in alignment with some investors, and they may not invest in your company. It is better to have this alignment early and avoid later conflict. At the same time, investors aligned to your Mission will be better partners for the company.
3. The Extended Enterprise: You and your channel partners, resellers, and suppliers will also benefit from being aligned with

your Mission. Your partners will usually go a bit farther for you if they know your purpose.

4. Customers: As the people who receive your products and services, your customers should experience your Mission rather than have it communicated to them. For example, your visit to Disneyland should make you happy; you do not need to be told about it.

Once the Mission is written down, it needs to be communicated well. Either explicitly or implicitly, a strong Mission Statement can help resolve divergent views between managers. It provides a balance against knee-jerk reactions, taken based on quarterly results, new opportunities, a wrong hire or market forces. Companies that remain true to their Mission, over time, significantly outperform those that do not.

> *A strong Mission Statement can help resolve divergent views within your organization.*

What is a Good Mission?

A Mission Statement should be an enduring statement of purpose and should be relatively unchanging over time. It must serve as a framework for evaluating the activities of an organization and to help resolve differences in strategy and direction. There is no definitive structure of a Mission Statement—it needs to work for the organization. There are, however, some guidelines for a good Mission Statement:

1. It must clearly state a purpose – the 'why' of an organization, and what it does. It must define what the organization is and what it will continue to be.
2. It should indicate the scope of activities that the organization will undertake and should allow for creative growth.

3. It should be short and stated in terms that can be unambiguously and widely understood by everyone in the organization.
4. It should stir emotions. Employees must be able to 'feel' the company Mission.
5. It should distinguish your organization from other similar ones.

Let us look at an example. Safetipin is an organization that provides safety-related data about public spaces to individuals and governments. Individuals use this information to take safer decisions, such as taking the safest route from one place to another. Governments use it for planning and to maintain infrastructure such as lighting. Safetipin collects this data from two sources. The first is by crowdsourcing through the MySafetipin app. The second is by using cameras placed in vehicles. Safetipin codifies this information through machine learning.

Their Mission— "Building a world where everyone can move around without fear, especially women."

1. The purpose of the organization is clearly identified in the entire statement.
2. The scope is the 'world', 'movement without fear', and 'everyone, especially women'. Today Safetipin provides data to make places safer. But putting the word 'data' into the Mission would limit its ability to perform other activities.
3. It is short enough to remember.
4. It certainly stirs emotions. 'Without fear' is a great articulation.
5. Safetipin is unique in the way it captures and provides data. It is distinguished from similar companies because of the focus on moving around without fear.

Another example is Flipkart. Their Mission is: "To provide our customers a memorable online shopping experience." Clear purpose, scope, and it is short and easy to remember. The word 'memorable' makes this Mission more than a bland statement of its business.

'Memorable' allows employees to align with its purpose and sets it up to be distinguished from others.

How to Uncover Your Mission Statement

Remember that the Mission is not about what you do as much as it is about why you do it. The reason already exists; it is a question of uncovering it. For a start-up, the reason will be best known to its founders. For a new department or project, the purpose should be obvious in its charter. In a company that has been in existence for a while, uncovering the Mission usually involves contribution from one or more board members, the CEO and maybe one or two key managers.

It is important to let a freshly minted Mission simmer for a few days. Perhaps something was missed out; perhaps it could be crafted better. The founder may want to share it with some of their trusted colleagues, to make sure it captures the essence of the organization. In some companies, the person responsible presents it to a group and invites comments and feedback. But when all the views are in, the final statement is decided by the CEO or the founders.

It is usually a good idea to document the discussions that led to the statement, and the meaning behind each phrase. This ensures that it does not get diluted or misinterpreted over time. Having it written down provides a way to refer to the original thought process.

Communicating the Mission

Once you have your Mission Statement, you may first want to prepare a slide deck. Whether you use the deck to address employees or not depends on your organization culture. But the slide deck will help in structuring the communication.

The deck should have three elements:

1. What a Mission Statement is and why your company needs one. Your employees need to understand how the Mission will be used and why it is relevant.

2. The process used in uncovering the Statement. To make the Statement come alive, employees need to understand that these words were carefully selected after considering many other options. Take them through the entire process including what was discarded and why.
3. Use stories explaining the Statement. The stories can be incidents that the founders went through which resulted in their deciding to start the company. Or other stories from within the organization.

After employees understand and connect with the Mission, it can be put up in places where it is visible and serves as a reminder.

The Mission Statement is often communicated beyond the employees of the company. It can be part of marketing collateral, presentations, the company website, and other external communications. Whenever you use your Mission Statement, add a small story to explain it and why it is appropriate for your company.

Vision: The Big Energizing Goal

While the Mission provides the purpose, the Vision of a company provides a picture of a destination in the foreseeable future. While the Mission does not change often and answers the question of 'why' the organization exists, the Vision provides a focus on something to be achieved. A Vision is usually time-bound. Once achieved or even nearly achieved, organizations can change their Vision to the next lodestone.

> *The Vision of a company provides a picture of a destination in the foreseeable future.*

A Vision Statement is hence an aspirational statement of what an organization would like to achieve. It is usually described in a single sentence. A good Vision can propel an organization, or even a country, to achieve the seemingly impossible. In 1960, during the peak of the Cold War with Russia, President John F Kennedy famously made a proclamation: "I believe that this nation should commit itself to achieving the goal, before this decade is out, to land a man on the moon and return him safely to earth." At that time, Russia was ahead in the Space Race. This Vision energized a nation and gave them something to be proud of. In achieving this goal, America moved ahead technologically, which has contributed in no small way to their continued dominance.

When it comes to companies, there are two types of Vision Statements. The first is a broad statement of ambition—like that of Sony who in the 1950s said that they would "become the company best known for changing the poor-quality image of Japanese products." While it is difficult to imagine today, in the 1960s, Japanese products were of poor quality. And Sony did lead in producing high-quality electronics and changing the image of Japanese products. This type of Vision is energising, but it does not commit to a specific goal.

There is a second type, like that of General Electric. In the seminal *Harvard Business Review (HBR)* article titled 'Building your Company's Vision' by Jim Collins and Jerry Poras, this type of Vision Statement was described as a BHAG (pronounced Bee-Hag). A BHAG is a 'Big Hairy Audacious Goal', one that can challenge a company to look beyond what they do at present, to what they can conceivably achieve. We will focus on BHAGs as Vision Statements.

General Electric or GE is one of the 50 largest companies in the world today—a conglomerate with a wide range of products and services, from aircraft engines to power generation, and industrial and financial products. In the 1980s, their Vision was to "Become the number 1 or number 2 in every market we serve." Since GE is a highly diversified company, this has reflected in many of the key decisions they have taken over the years, whether it was their acquisition of Alstom's Power and Grid business or the divestment of their appliances business to Haier and hiving off Synchrony Financials.

Some Vision Statements are of relatively short duration. In 2012, YouTube set their BHAG to reach a viewership of one billion user hours every day by 2016. By 2014, well into their deadline, they had reached about 100M hours of viewership every day. The target looked completely out of reach. In those two years, however, it became their all-consuming passion. It touched every part of the organization including their strategy of changing their cloud infrastructure and marketing in fundamental ways. They made their goal with a month to spare.

Why is a Vision Important?

While the Mission provides a purpose, the Vision provides a focus and a goal. The Vision should be hard to achieve but should be possible. It should be a worthwhile goal—one that everyone in the organization can relate to. More than the Mission, the Vision is the specific and visible lodestar that drives organization processes and goals.

As companies grow and achieve their initial Vision, they should re-evaluate and set a new Vision. Airtel is one of the top telecom companies in India and a leader in the transformation of mobile services for two decades, starting from the mid-1990s. In the year 2000, their Vision was: "We will make mobile communications a way of life and be the customers' first choice." Mobile phones were not as ubiquitous as they are today, and a local call was expensive. It was a bold statement at the time—making a mobile phone a 'way of life' was too distant a goal.

But a scant six years later, it seemed trivial; mobile phone penetration in major cities was more than 90%. So, in 2006, Airtel revised its Vision to "By 2010, Airtel will be the most admired brand in India, loved by more customers, targeted by top talent, benchmarked by more businesses." Airtel had set its sights on becoming a premier brand in the country and started focusing on long-term sustainable growth.

So, while a Mission provides purpose and meaning, a Vision provides focus and results in action.

What is a Good Vision?

Like a good Mission, the Vision should be easy to understand and remember. It does not have a specific structure, just one that is most suitable for an organization. At the same time, there are specific guidelines for a good Vision Statement:

1. It must be a Big Hairy Audacious Goal—it should clearly state 'what' the primary focus of the organization should be.
2. It should reflect the organization's measures of success. This should be a primary indicator of the organization's success.
3. It should be vivid and inspiring. The Vision should paint a vivid picture of a future desirable state, one that inspires people.
4. It should be realistic and have at least a tenuous visible path. There is rarely a specific path to the Vision, but it should not be

completely unachievable. There must be some visible way to get there so that it is believable.

5. It should be short and should be stated in terms that can be unambiguous and widely understood by everyone.

Let us look at an example. In 2019, ESRI India became a wholly owned subsidiary of ESRI, the global leader in Geographic Information System (GIS). With about 70% of the market share in an industry that was growing at 13%, ESRI India was a healthy successful entity, with substantial influence in GIS policy. For them, a vivid future was to step outside the comfort zone of proprietary server-based solutions. They had to move from largely government applications into newer areas.

Their Vision reflected that: "1 million ESRI users by 2024." That is a big leap for a company with 25,000 users. In five years, they plan to increase the number of licensed users of ESRI software in India by a factor of 40 times. This will require a massive increase in the number of GIS users in the country. So ESRI is effectively committing to change the way GIS software is used and the applications they are used for. A simple but bold statement.

Let us see if it meets all the criteria

1. It is certainly an audacious goal.
2. It is a key and transformational measure of success for the organization.
3. It is vivid and inspiring; it takes use of GIS software out of the realm of a few into widespread usage.
4. There was a lot of discussion about whether it was realistic and feasible. But by the end, the team believed it could be done.
5. It is certainly short and clear.

ESRI India primarily targets specific applications within government departments. To reach their goal of a million users, they will need to discover new avenues for revenue and perhaps new business models as well.

Creating Your Vision Statement

Usually the senior management team of an organization creates the Vision. When the Vision is effective, it is Big Hairy and Audacious. Hence the creation process is often both exhilarating and somewhat scary. A comfortable and achievable goal is not a Vision.

> *When the Vision is effective, it is Big Hairy and Audacious. It is often both exhilarating and somewhat scary.*

To be effective, the team must step out well beyond their area of comfort and visualize a future that is quite different from where they are today. Most teams are not able to make the leap in their first attempt. Initial Vision Statements tend to be grand but vague, and often do not cause significant change.

The Vision Statement is usually crafted in a facilitated workshop for the top management team. They start by envisioning their future both within and outside the context of their industry. It is useful to have some guiding questions to help the discussion along. Each participant writes a short story based on the question.

Here is an example of a question.

"The day is five years from today. Your company has just received an award, one that signals a major milestone in the company's history. You are making a short speech to your employees explaining the award and its importance. What will you say?"

The time frame should usually be something outside the regular planning horizon, so people are required to use their imagination, but not so far out that their imagination becomes fanciful. Each story conjures an image. A facilitated discussion around these images generates ideas for the Vision Statement.

The team must then be able to see at least a part of the path to getting there. It may involve resources beyond those that are currently available. It must be both possible and exciting; ambitious, but not ridiculous. Usually, the sign of a good Vision Statement is when the people in the room are both energized by its boldness and a bit nervous about how they will get there.

When Do You Change Your Vision?

There are a few reasons to reconsider your Vision Statement:

1. Substantial changes in the market or the environment that makes the Vision irrelevant, unachievable or too easy to achieve. For example, the entry of low-cost Chinese phones made the market-share growth vision of an Indian manufacturer impossible to achieve.
2. You have achieved your Vision, or it is no longer challenging.
3. You set an overambitious Vision and cannot see a path to meeting it.
4. You realize that the measure itself was not the right one for you. For example, a device manufacturer set a goal of selling a certain number of units of their product, and later introduced many other product categories. They changed their measure to be revenue instead.

You can re-examine your Vision during your annual planning cycle. If there is a need to change it, do it at that time.

When communicating the change, explain the reason for needing to change it, and the process that will be followed to do so.

Leveraging the Vision Statement

The Vision Statement is best communicated along with the Mission Statement. Even when the Vision changes, the Mission continues to provide the guiding force for the Vision. The approach to communication remains the same as that of the Mission Statement.

In addition to communication, the Vision Statement is used during planning to set individual and team goals.

Core Strategy: How You Will Win

Strategy is a plan of action to achieve a long-term or overall goal.

The word Strategy originates in the military but has now become common parlance in the business world. We now have marketing strategy, development strategy or even a specific customer strategy. Any person seeking to understand strategy can be subject to a bewildering number of interpretations of the word.

The purpose of a Core Strategy is to build a sustainable 'moat' around your business. The moat helps defend the business against your competitors. Hence the Core Strategy is about sustainable and profitable differentiation; how your organization will be more profitable and will grow faster than your competitors. While the Mission is the 'why' of the business and the Vision is the 'what', the Core Strategy is the 'how'.

In this chapter, we will focus on the critical elements of a Core Strategy. It is the interplay of the elements of your business that will ensure that you grow, while at the same time it will build a defensive 'moat' around your business. The template we will create is simple, and in the real world it will usually be accompanied with data analysis and modelling to explain the rationale.

Types of Businesses

Pipeline Businesses

Most businesses depend on a sequential flow of activities from research to manufacturing, sales, distribution and after-sales services. This is known as the value chain—a set of processes that generate value. They are sequential; hence the term pipeline.

Strategy models for pipeline businesses are subject to market forces in a way that has been best descried by Michael Porter. He postulates five forces that determine competitive strategy. An outline of these five forces is provided in Annexure 1.

Businesses achieve scale and competitive advantage through controlling supply side economics. Pipeline businesses focus on efficiency and lowering their costs so that they are more profitable than their competitors. They erect barriers for others to enter into their industry, and they set up their value chain to be exclusive wherever possible. They scale by sourcing at a low cost, setting up infrastructure that is hard to replicate and providing price advantages to their customers.

Walmart creates a moat by providing consistently lower prices for a variety of products as compared to other retailers. They can do this because their sales volumes allows them to negotiate better rates with their suppliers. Their presence raises footfall, which allows them to negotiate low rentals for their stores.

Platform Businesses

The increased sophistication and availability of technology to all strata of society in the past few decades has changed the traditional models of business success. New entrants with similar products can access global manufacturing capability; social media provides targeted access to customers; and cloud computing solutions provide access to sophisticated systems without them having to build their own infrastructure.

This has provided opportunities to businesses that facilitate transactions between stakeholders. Companies that connect customers to providers have emerged as new leaders in the marketplace. These are known as platform businesses.

Platform businesses create value for both the consumers and the providers of services. As their ecosystem grows, the value of their network increases for both consumers and providers. This is the 'network effect'. As the size of the network grows, it generates more value for all the members of the network. For example, as more people use Google's Android platform, it attracts more developers; and as the number of users of an application increase, more phone manufacturers and other users are attracted to it.

Platform businesses grow through demand side economics. Comparative studies show that they grow faster, and they have better margins and higher valuations as compared to similar pipeline businesses. Since they do not own physical infrastructure, they are more agile and can quickly leverage the capabilities of other providers in their network.

Platform businesses compete with each other, just like pipeline businesses do. They have to contend with 'multihoming', where customers use more than one platform and may switch from one to another. Facebook, Google, Alibaba, Tencent, Uber and Airbnb are all examples of successful platforms.

Hybrid Businesses

Hybrid businesses combine elements of pipeline and platform businesses. They set up ecosystems while also building physical infrastructure. Amazon has its own products and distribution network, and Apple has both its own products and a comprehensive ecosystem that develops applications. They have the benefits and risks of the other two business approaches.

Is There a Recommended Model for Business?

While successful platform businesses have higher valuation, they facilitate their providers and customers. As such, they will always be much smaller in number when compared to pipeline businesses. They are also more expensive to set up and have higher risk.

However, there are valuable lessons for pipeline businesses to learn from platform businesses:

1. Leverage platforms for your business. Platforms make it easier to reach customers, and to lower barriers. For example, if

you have a clothing line, platforms make it easier to reach to customers interested in purchasing your products.
2. Interact more deeply with your customers. Platforms use data extensively to understand customer preferences. Tracking customer use of your products and services will help you understand them better.

The Five Elements of Core Strategy

Whether your business is a pipeline, platform or hybrid, there will be five key elements to your Core Strategy.

- Premise: What is your simple business concept? Do you have a key insight that can differentiate you from your competitors?
- Proposition: What is the unique and differentiated value that you bring to your customers?
- Provisioning: How will you uniquely fulfil your customers' needs?
- Penetration: How will you increase your reach, revenues and profits?
- Perimeter: What is the scope of your business? What will you not do?

To explain these elements, we will look at two pipeline examples and one platform example.

- Ikea is the world's largest furniture retailer. It targets young furniture buyers with a sense of style but who have a low budget and smaller homes.
- Milkbasket delivers select groceries. It targets nuclear families living in gated communities where both parents are working.
- Betterplace is a platform that connects blue-collar workers, companies that employ them and companies that provide services to workers.

Premise

The Premise of your business identifies why your business will be successful, and it should ideally be based on two things.

The first is a unique and actionable insight to your customer needs. In the 1950s, Dick and Mac worked out ways to make the cuisine in their restaurant consistent. They developed a range of equipment, including a dispenser that would squirt the same amount of ketchup and mustard every time and a rotating platform that would speed up the process of making a burger. Their unique insight was that customers wanted predictability at a low price. Macdonald's did to food what Ford did to automobiles.

> *The 'Premise' identifies why your business will be successful. It should be based on an actionable customer insight*

More recently, Amazon's insight was that customers would choose convenience over the sensory approach of a shopping experience. Apple has a clear understanding that their customers want a simple yet elegant experience, and they would be willing to pay for it.

The second is the economic engine: how the company will make a profit. Focusing on standardization and quality allowed Macdonald's to be highly profitable and also to become the earliest restaurant franchise. Amazon makes money through both a hugely efficient distribution network and a percentage of all partner sales. Apple has monetized its entire ecosystem, with their customers wedded to the range of products and services they offer.

Let's see the Premise behind our three companies.

Ikea

1. Ikea's unique insight is that their customers would be willing to make a lot of effort to get nicely designed furniture at a reasonable price.

2. By making their furniture modular and requiring customers to take it home and assemble it, Ikea was able to reduce their unit cost significantly enough to make a higher profit with a lower price point.

Milkbasket

1. Milkbasket's unique insight is that their customers like to have their regular groceries at their doorstep whenever they wake up in the morning.
2. By delivering only to dense clusters of residences, allowing families to set up regular deliveries and taking prepayment with no returns, Milkbasket's delivery costs are a fraction of their competitors'.

Betterplace

1. Betterplace's unique insight at their founding, was that records of blue-collar and migrant workers were not accurately available to employers.
2. Betterplace started by charging employers for fast and reliable employee verification, and over time they increased the range of services to address the entire lifecycle of managing a blue-collar workforce, from sourcing, to hiring, onboarding, attendance, and payroll. They are now letting other service providers provide solutions such as insurance, personal loans, vehicle loans and training to enhance worker skills. In all cases, they have taken a different approach from their competitors.

A clear and simple business concept can lead to a highly differentiated strategy.

Proposition

The Proposition is the promise of a set of benefits that customers will receive. Over time, this should be delivered by you, and should be accepted and acknowledged by your customers. At some point, the Proposition becomes the brand of the company.

> *The 'Proposition' identifies the (preferably unique) set of benefits that your customers will receive from you. It should resonate with your actionable customer insight.*

In many of the best companies, the actionable customer insight and their Proposition come together seamlessly. For example, Apple's Proposition can be summed up as "The experience IS the product." This is also their by-line, and it brings all their devices and ecosystem together in the mind of the customer.

In 2007, two roommates, Joe and Brian were having a hard time meeting their rent payments. Coincidently, their city was hosting a large design conference with many delegates needing affordable accommodation. They bought three air mattresses, put them in their loft apartment and put up a website to advertise the availability of a place to stay. They offered breakfast and city tours as well. Their insight was that people travelling on business would pay to stay at homes if they were conveniently located. They also discovered that many people were happy to make their homes available for short rentals. The company they started—Airbnb.

Being a platform, Airbnb has two types of customers. The first are the people who need a place to stay. The Proposition to them is both a lower cost as well as a unique experience every time, but with assurance of quality. The second type are homeowners who want to rent out their properties. For them, the Proposition is additional income from their houses or properties.

Let us see the Proposition for each of our three selected companies.

In the case of Ikea,

- The Proposition for their customer is great design and wide variety for a reasonable cost.

In the case of Milkbasket,

- The Proposition for their customer is that they can place repeatable orders for items like milk and bread, with the convenience that the order will be outside their door in the morning.

In the case of Betterplace, as a platform, there are three sides to their business:

- For the consumer (the blue-collar worker), the Proposition is to find employment and receive services tailored specifically for them.
- For the employer, the value proposition is worker verification, hiring workers with required skills, worker satisfaction and reduction of operational costs.
- For businesses with services for blue-collar workers, the value proposition is both access and authentication.

Provisioning

Provisioning differs substantially between pipeline and platform businesses.

For pipeline businesses, the value chain is the process or activities by which a company builds and delivers a product or experience. This includes logistics, production, marketing, and the provision of after-sales services. A successful pipeline business model usually tunes its processes to uniquely meet their customer proposition. This helps deepen the moat around the business and protect it from competition.

In platform businesses, Provisioning is often about a better user experience. What to display, where to display it, how easy it is to use, and supporting features are all important elements. The moat here comes from data. Platforms collect data about their customers and then use this data to personalize their experience. Amazon recommends purchases, Netflix recommends shows and TikTok serves content based on what users like.

There are also hybrid businesses that have elements of both. Let us look at Amazon. It has many suppliers on the platform, which makes it appealing to buyers. However, they also do logistics and delivery of goods directly to the customer, which is a pipeline element to its platform. This increases the value of the platform to both the buyer and the seller since Amazon assures timely and safe delivery.

> *'Provisioning' identifies the key (preferably unique) ways in which you will deliver your product or service to your customer.*

Let us look at how Ikea, Milkbasket and Betterplace do it.

- In the case of Ikea, it starts from design. Their furniture is designed so that it can be shipped in boxes. Their manufacturing and packaging follow suit. They have warehouses located on the outskirts of cities where the costs are low, and their product displays are minimal. However, they have a great loading area and an excellent food counter. They even provide childcare facilities to allow their customers to select furniture without stress. They provide a holistic nuclear family experience.
- In the case of Milkbasket, their logistics are highly optimized. Their delivery staff usually do this as a second job for a few hours in the morning. Since they deliver to fewer and more concentrated areas, their costs of fuel are lower. By delivering during non-peak hours, they can do their deliveries faster with less traffic. And by not accepting cash and delivering outside the door, they have reduced logistical complexity as well as the number of returns. They are now turning their focus to sourcing and warehousing innovation to further improve their quality and reduce costs.
- In the case of Betterplace, they have a very efficient process for worker verification, which is done physically through a network of associates. They customize their platform for organizations and integrate it with their existing systems. They personalize job recommendations for workers based on their available data. As part of their roadmap, as more service providers become

available on their platform, they will drive higher engagement with their blue collared workforce.

Penetration

Penetration is the part of Core Strategy that looks at your approach to growth. This usually involves decisions around products and markets. The Ansoff Matrix is probably the simplest and most elegant way of viewing growth options for moving into new markets or new products. The Ansoff Matrix is shown in the figure given here.

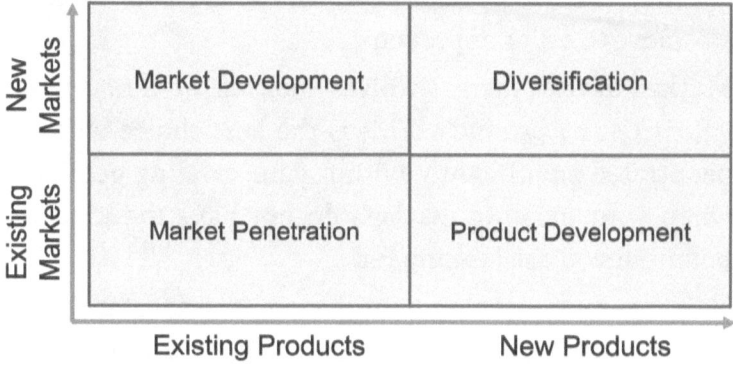

> *'Penetration' is the element of Core Strategy that looks at how your company will grow. This usually involves decisions on products and markets.*

Companies can implement more than one of the approaches, but only one of the ones chosen is usually the primary approach.

- Market penetration refers to increasing business from a geography where the company is already strong and with existing products. This is the best option when the existing market for your products is large and you have a defensible competitive position. This approach has the lowest cost of fulfilment and hence is often the most profitable.

- Most pipeline businesses start with a narrow market for their product or service to get customer feedback and then find the best ways of reaching customers. Companies in some industries, like telecom, remain in this phase, because of regulation and high capex involved.
- Platform business may start here, especially when they already have competition. Facebook, for example, was released within Harvard and was then adopted by other universities before expanding. However, by their nature, they are not limited by geographical boundaries and will move to other approaches.
- Market development involves looking at new markets with your existing products. This is the best choice when you have penetrated significantly within your existing geographies and when your existing markets do not have the kind of growth potential you are looking for.
- New product development becomes important when your existing products have reached maturity and face a declining market share or are already saturated with your existing product. Since you are already present in the market, it is easy to test new products and introduce them.
  - For pipeline businesses, product development usually involves adding products that your existing customers would want. It helps compete more effectively when adding to a family of products. For example, adding different flavours to chips can cater to a wider audience while improving brand awareness.
  - For platform businesses, this involves additional features that can engage customers better, for instance, Whatsapp adding voice calling in 2015 and increasing their usage substantially. New features add loyalty and reduce multi-homing, which is a term to describe customers using multiple similar platforms.

- Diversification requires you to look for areas outside your current range of products and markets. This usually happens when your existing products have reached the end of their life cycle or have been significantly disrupted. Often, your existing brand and customers will not support new products from you. It usually signals a major shift in the functioning of a company and is hence the last choice.

A critical element of platform businesses is deciding which side of the platform to grow first and which side to monetize. In any new city, Uber first grows the driver side through incentives so that customers can find cabs when they want them. Over time, they take a part of the fee paid by the customer. Facebook held off any form of monetization till it had a large customer base and then monetized through advertising and later through service providers.

> *A critical element of platform businesses is deciding which side of the platform to grow first and which side to monetize.*

Let us see the implications of the Core Strategy for growth for our three companies.

- Ikea's presence in their existing markets is strong, and they have a remarkably high share of their target group. Hence their primary growth strategy is Market Development.
- Milkbasket's primary growth strategy is Market Penetration. Once Milkbasket identifies an area, it attempts to get a high percentage of the customers in that area.
- Betterplace's primary growth strategy is Product Development. They are continually building new services on top of workforce data on their platform to help companies manage and engage their workers better. Adding new services from service providers makes their platform richer for both blue collar workers and their employers.

Having identified the primary growth strategy, you should also identify the approach to acquire customers. There is a wide range of approaches, from having a sales team, to using sales channels, local marketing events, advertising and online engagement. Many companies use a combination of these approaches.

Both Ikea and MilkBasket use hyperlocal approaches to access customers, which includes local advertising and promotions.

- When looking at new markets, Ikea first commissions a study to understand the design sensibilities of that market and to see how compatible that market is to their value proposition. Ikea's growth comes from adding new warehouses and then increasing the throughput from that warehouse. Ikea's first warehouse in India is in Hyderabad and they are promoting their 1,000-seater restaurant as much as they promote their furniture.
- MilkBasket promotes their products through hyperlocal online advertising, newspaper inserts and notices. They are increasing their number of customers within each defined area, so their costs are always optimized. If they are not able to get a certain number of customers within a defined period, they withdraw services to ensure profitability.
- Betterplace approaches organizations through a select business development team. Once an organization signs up for their services, their blue-collar workers are integrated into the platform. Their first side for growth is the blue-collar worker, so they also reach out directly through social media channels to workers not presently employed with their customers. They offer access to job opportunities and skill training. They monetize the organization side and the service provider side. However, their consumer side (blue-collar workers) services are at no cost.

Perimeter

Core Strategy is about choices. It is important to know what to do, but it is equally important to know what not to do. It is about differentiation;

about providing a value proposition (product, service, or combination) that is different from your competitors and then putting together unique processes that allow for increased profit. Core Strategy means constantly obsessing about customer behaviour and ensuring that your proposition and processes keep pace with their changing needs.

> *Setting your 'Perimeter' means making choices about what not to do.*

Ikea does not customize. They do not change fabric, colour or materials based on personal choice. This is not because they do not recognize these as important considerations for people. They choose to provide people with great design at an affordable cost and making changes will change that balance. Hence it does not fit into their Core Strategy.

- Milkbasket does not deliver at any time outside the morning and does not accept cash payments at the time of delivery. They also recognize that not all customers want deliveries outside their door, and many want to pay cash. But doing this will increase their costs and will not allow them to compete effectively.
- Betterplace does not extend their services to workers outside the blue-collar space. While a few employers have been interested in extending their services to all employees, Betterplace stays very clearly focused on their segment.

These choices have kept these companies focused and have helped to ensure their growth and improve their profitability to much higher levels as compared to the industry.

What is a Good Core Strategy?

The primary goal of a business is its Vision—a Big Hairy Audacious Goal, along with a few others including revenue and profit. The Core Strategy provides clarity on how exactly this will happen. Always remember that the Core Strategy must help define clearly how to win in a competitive environment.

A good Core Strategy does the following:

1. Clearly identifies the target customer(s) who will buy your product or service.
2. Has a simple overarching business Premise that is ideally based on a unique and actionable insight about your customer—one that they (or someone else) are willing to pay for at a price higher than your cost to produce and deliver your product or service.
3. Is specific and differentiated about the Proposition. Why should the customer choose your product of service over similar products or services? Is it because you have the best product, most choice, best price or best service, or are most convenient? If your business is a platform, you need to answer this question for all sides of your business.
4. Is differentiated in the Provisioning of products and services, so that your value chain can be operated at a lower cost to deliver your Proposition. The traditional value chain consists of Research & Development, Logistics, Manufacturing, Fulfilment, Sales and Marketing, and Customer Service. Companies that optimize all elements of their value chain to deliver a unique proposition usually have a sustainable advantage and deliver long-term results.
5. Has a clearly articulated position for growth, whether to focus on penetration, market development, product development or diversification. This then leads to an approach for addressing the market.
6. Makes choices of what not to do. It is always tempting to add new pieces to the offering, but it reduces focus, usually increases cost and complexity, often without proportional increased value in the eyes of the customer.

7. Is aligned to changing customer preferences. Are others offering your customers better or different options? Are they veering away from your offering (or even thinking about it)? If so, relook at all the elements of your Core Strategy.

Representing Your Core Strategy: The Strategy Map

Every company has a Core Strategy, whether it is articulated or not. If you have not represented it clearly in the past, you may have a complex set of Core Strategies. Unless you are starting a new company, many elements of the Core Strategy will already be in place. A Strategy Map is a simple format to articulate your Core Strategy.

The example given here is a possible articulation of the Strategy Map for Ikea.

Strategy Map

Customer	Premise
Young adults who have small budgets, small homes, but like style	Customers will pick up and assemble their own furniture if the price and design is right
Proposition: A wide range of well-designed, functional home furnishing products at prices so low that as many people as possible will be able to afford them.	
Provisioning: Value Chain:	
Design → Manufacturing → Sales Outlets → Sales & Marketing → Customer Support	
• Design. Contemporary, international designs, that can be assembled easily • Sales Outlets. Large stores providing nuclear families with a day-out experience • Sales & Marketing. Local marketing of furniture and experience	
Penetration: Growth	**Perimeter: Will not do**
Market Development: Select the right city based on costs and demographic. Set up store while doing extensive hyperlocal content-based marketing.	• Any customization • Furniture that cannot be shipped in a box • Direct delivery to customer

Developing and Updating Your Core Strategy

Your Core Strategy is relatively unchanging, and it works on continuing differentiation to meet customer requirements. You may however be in a business where not all the elements mentioned earlier are presently differentiated. Many companies work on these elements over time to build their competitive advantage.

Preparing the As-is Document

The Strategy Map is a simple format and can serve as a template to be filled in. A single session with the CEO of your company is usually enough to complete the elements required for the template. All companies have a Core Strategy. This step is to document it.

There are usually four challenges in completing the document:

1. Mixing tactical or operational elements in strategy. For example, outsourcing non-core activities is not a Core Strategy.
2. Mixing what the Core Strategy is with what it should be. In the first document, try and be brutally honest.
3. Having multiple approaches to some sections. That is fine. Leave them all in.
4. A temporary recency bias. Actions taken to counter an economic downturn or perhaps a competitor campaign should not show up in the Core Strategy.

Answering the Tough Questions

While all elements of Core Strategy are required, there are a few that are harder than others and need a deep understanding:

1. Are we sure we have the right customer identified? If not, who should it be?
2. Do we have a unique and actionable insight about our customers' needs? If not, can we find one?
3. Is our company tuned to deliver our unique proposition better than anyone else? Which processes or methods can get us there?

You need an open mind while answering these questions, and the answers may be uncomfortable. If you find that you do not have answers that you are satisfied with, it is important to get those satisfactory answers.

A small team that includes the CEO and a few senior managers can have a few sessions together. Between these sessions, each person will need to speak to the customers, research all the options, study the market and global trends, study their competitors and work with others internally to think through new processes.

Alternatively, an external consultant can work with the management team or take the mandate to come up with the answers to these questions.

This process may take several months. Many tools are useful in thinking through these questions. Some of the tools frequently used are covered in Appendix 1.

Completing the New Strategy Map

Once the three critical questions are answered, a single participatory workshop with the team involved in answering the first few questions is usually adequate to complete the rest of the Strategy Map.

The new Strategy Map must then be implemented. This is usually done through a series of strategic initiatives. A good way to do that is covered in the next section of this book.

Updating the Strategy Map

As your company gets bigger and your strategy becomes more nuanced, you should do a formal exercise once a year to update your Core Strategy. This can be combined with your annual planning exercise.

This is usually done as a management workshop. People within the company are charted to make presentations on the following:

1. Market and environment: Look at the size of the market, and how fast it is growing or shrinking. Evaluate the environmental factors at play that can impact your Core Strategy. Look at new ideas and research that could disrupt the existing market, specifically around technology.
2. Competition: It is useful to study four types of competitors.
   a. Those who provide a similar product or platform to your customer segments.
   b. Those that offer 'substitutes'—alternate products to meet a similar customer need.
   c. Those that are providing a solution like yours but to another customer set.
   d. New entrants into your market who may have disruptive solutions.
3. Customers and Changing Preferences: This should include results from feedback surveys, focus groups and in-depth interviews. Your study should look for insights of customer buying behaviour or changes in their buying behaviour including win/loss analysis.
4. Internal performance: Look at how the company has performed vis-à-vis the plans and growth over the years. There should be a specific focus on your value chain and whether it remains distinctive, effective and efficient.

These presentations should be followed by a SWOT[1] (Strengths, Weaknesses, Opportunities and Threats) table.

The annual study of the market, competition, customers and internal performance should focus on insights, and not on data aggregation.

---

1   SWOT Analysis is outlined in Annexure 1

> *When developing or modifying Core Strategy, the study of the market, competition, customers and internal performance, should focus on insights, and not on data aggregation.*

After the presentations, the team should decide which of the insights are worth focusing on. Since a lot of the focus is on potential changes, a healthy mix of scepticism and paranoia is required while assessing the environment and internal processes. It is possible that an insight that was ignored one year is accepted the following year.

The insights that are finally selected are then considered to see how they impact the Core Strategy. This is done by applying each insight to the six key questions.

- Is there a change in our customer profile?
- Is there a need to change our simple business premise?
- Do we need to modify our value proposition (for each customer type)?
- Is our value chain still distinctive? What should we do to further improve it?
- Is there a need to change our growth model?
- What will we not do?

The answers to the questions are then used to update the Strategy Map.

Where Are You Going? Epilogue

The first workshop for Livewell was scheduled on a Saturday. It was the first day when all four of them were free and Javed was also available.

They started with their Mission Statement right away. "We need to answer the question "What is our purpose at Livewell?" said Javed. "Why do we exist?"

"Well, I guess we do want to be a company that is big and profitable," said Subodh.

"That's a reason any company exists. What's the real purpose behind Livewell?" Javed responded.

"How about to transform the healthcare industry?" said Ankit.

"It's a bit broad, but it works," said Javed. "Our purpose should engage our heart, not our head. We should be able to feel it. Let's address this another way. Why don't each of you share your story of why you started Livewell. Ankit, would you like to start?"

"OK," said Ankit. "Subodh knows this story, but it will be new for the rest of you. During my first year at IIT, my father had a heart attack. He recovered, but my family went through a traumatic time. The doctors told us that if my father had done his regular annual check-ups, this could have been detected earlier and prevented."

Subodh nodded. "I was with Ankit when he got the news of his father's heart attack. When I learned from Ankit that it could have been prevented, we discussed that there had to be a simple solution. So, later when it was time to do a project, we decided to build a wearable device with sensors."

This story generated resonance within the team. Over the next few hours, they agreed on their new Mission Statement: "We alert to prevent medical emergencies." This resonated with all of them. The sense of purpose and coherence in the room was palpable.

"I think you have nailed it," said Javed. "This Statement is energizing, has purpose, is easy to remember, is a perfect fit and provides clear direction."

Kamini nodded. "This feels right."

Javed continued. "Our next step is to define our Vision—our Big Hairy Audacious Goal. Think five years into the future. Where do you see yourselves?"

"The Prime Minister of India should be wearing a Livewell device," said Kamini.

Everyone laughed. "That is certainly an interesting Vision and would prove that Livewell has reached a level of popularity where even the Prime Minister would wear it," said Javed.

"I was just joking," smiled Kamini.

"Given that we are looking at something big," Kriti said, "should we look at a certain number of wearables that we would have in the next few years?"

"That's interesting," said Subodh. "How about five times in five years. That would be 40% growth each year."

"We are presently projecting to grow by over 60% next year, so while we may slow down going forward, this does not seem to be big enough. At our projected run rate, we will grow ten times in five years," said Ankit.

"That's five million wearables," said Kriti. "Assuming the market continues to grow the way it has been, it would make us the biggest wearable company in India by a big margin."

Ankit looked thoughtful. "That does seem a bit of a stretch, given that a number of Chinese options are available already at a much lower price point. But what if we grow globally? Then this number seems to be rather low. What if we look at ten million wearables in five years?"

Everyone was quiet.

"Well that sucked the energy from the room," joked Kamini.

"It's crazy but possible," said Subodh. "It would put us comfortably within the top ten global wearables. From a product capability angle, we are already there. We will need to think about everything else very differently though. Our distribution, marketing, partnerships, everything will need to change. It's an exciting thought."

"You will also need to raise a lot more money," said Kriti. "The interesting thing is that Livewell has been able to execute their plans pretty well till now, and it may be possible to raise the money if we have a good plan."

Javed was smiling. "It's a good sign when your Vision is big enough to cause excitement with a hint of panic."

Ankit looked at Subodh. "Let's do it!"

Everyone nodded. They agreed to meet again in a few days along with others from the senior team at Livewell to come up with their Core Strategy.

Over the next few days, Ankit and Subodh shared Livewell's Mission and Vision with their senior managers and in a town hall meeting. Everyone loved the simplicity and clarity they represented. Ankit and Subodh both shared not just the statements but also what it meant and how they came up with it. There were many questions, but everyone was supportive.

Javed engaged with other senior managers to prepare for the Core Strategy workshop. There were a dozen people present at the workshop.

The workshop started with a set of presentations. The marketing head presented the different customer segments using Livewell, and their priorities. Subodh presented the SWOT (Strengths, Weaknesses, Opportunities and Threats) for Livewell. Ankit presented the analysis of global marketplace and what their competitors were doing. The head of R&D presented features from wearables around the world, new research on sensors and what they were working on.

Javed then explained what a Core Strategy was all about. He explained the 5Ps of Core Strategy that would together differentiate Livewell from the competition. For the next few hours, the group split into three teams to work on their competitive advantage.

The discussions were eye-opening for the entire team. They discovered that they were trying too many different approaches to get ahead. They were being opportunistic—chasing each opportunity till the next one came along.

They realized that they had two major customer segments that were vital for their business. The first were the general physicians in clinics and hospitals who could use their data and recommend the device. The second were wearable users. They agreed that their target end-users were men and women between the ages of 40 years and 55 years with a largely sedentary lifestyle.

Kamini said, "I am now a bit confused. Up until today, our major competitor was always Fitbit. But they are targeting a younger demographic and people who are or want to be fit. That is not what we are doing at all. So, if these are our customer segments, who exactly is our competition?"

Javed added, "That's a good point. And we may not have an exact competitor today. What we may have a blue ocean idea—one that is a completely new way of looking at the market. Let's just try and plot your Strategy Canvas."

Kriti raised her hand. "That's all very well, but I have no idea what either 'blue ocean' or 'strategy canvas' mean."

"Sorry," Javed laughed embarrassedly. "I got carried away. The idea of a blue ocean was introduced by W. Chan Kim and Renee Mauborgne. The central idea is that most markets are red oceans with a lot of competition, where the rule is the survival of the fittest, or a lot of blood in the water. A blue ocean on the other hand is one where you find or create a space that does not have any competition, and you have a unique way to occupy it.

In their book, *Blue Ocean Strategy'* the authors use a tool called the Strategy Canvas to identify elements of a product that can take it to a blue ocean. Rather than explain it, let's just build it. It will become clear as we work on it."

"Got it," said Kriti. "Let's get started."

Over the next hour, the group came up with their Strategy Canvas.

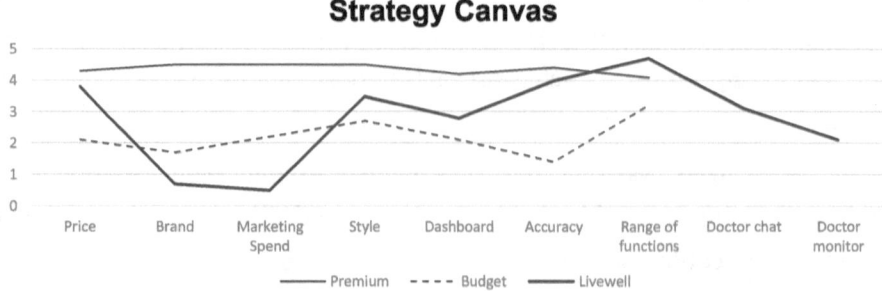

Premium and budget devices were plotted first. As expected, their value parameters followed expected lines. As a start-up, Livewell had a lower brand presence and marketing spend, but the highest range of functions.

"If you want to create a new market, you should focus on the value that others don't have. That's the ability for your customers to chat with their doctor and monitor their scores based on the levels set by their doctor. Your product focus should be to push up your rating on those two values," said Javed.

"This is interesting," said Subodh. "We are providing a medical device, but so far have been addressing the market like it's a lifestyle device. We need to think about our market differently."

"That's right," said Ankit. "If we look at Livewell as a medical device, we have a unique position. We should be focusing on our ecosystem with our wearable at the centre. This is a real breakthrough. I need a break to process this. Let's step out for a cup of coffee."

They walked to the nearest gourmet coffee place. Discussions continued around their new discovery and how it cleared up so much. Javed had been quiet for most of it. "You know, this may be even more significant than you think. We should now be thinking of ourselves as a platform business."

Kamini asked, "What does that mean? Are we not a platform business anyway? What does this change?"

Kriti added. "Let me try this. A platform business is when a company facilitates exchanges between two interdependent groups. So, if we are connecting doctors and possible patients through our wearable and technology, we are essentially following a platform business model."

"That's interesting," said Subodh, "but it does not really change any discussions we have been having so far, does it?"

"Well, yes and no," said Javed, who had earlier nodded in acceptance of Kriti's statement. "While the approach we are following is the same, there are some nuances we should keep in mind. Right now, we could perhaps worry about two things. The first is the Network effect. The nature of a platform is that its value increases as each new person joins the network."

"Does that mean that as people buying a Livewell wearable increases, the value increases? I don't really see why that is a big deal. As any product grows, their quality becomes better and the brand stronger, which will add value to new buyers," said Subodh.

Ankit was looking thoughtful. "I think what you are saying is that as the number of doctors increase, the value to our wearable users increase, since they are likely to have someone who can use their data, and as the number of users increase, doctors will find it more valuable to learn about and use Livewell."

"That's exactly right," said Javed. "And that brings me to the second thing you perhaps need to worry about right now, and that is the chicken-and-egg situation. Which comes first, the doctor or the user?"

"Hmmm, I see what you are saying," said Kamini. "There needs to be a critical mass of one, so that it attracts the other. Currently, most of our customers are wearable users. Maybe we should double down and establish that first. Then we can go to doctors with a better story."

"I'm actually thinking we should go the other way," said Ankit. "We double down on signing up doctors and incentivize them in some way. They may recommend a few users to buy it. Once we have done that, we do a social media push using quotes from doctors to try and convince users to buy Livewell devices."

Subodh was nodding. "That makes sense to me too. In fact, our wearable is already modular. We can give doctors the option to select the sensors they need for each patient."

Kriti added, "As long as we are talking about two sides to the network, we may want to consider a third. We do not have to limit our sensors only to the ones we have access to. We should be open to partnerships with others, to incorporate their sensors either into our product or as a co-branded product on our platform."

Ankit said, "Wow Kriti, that's really cool. This will increase the network effect and will be a great deal both for us and the other providers. I love it. Our platform today is not yet ready, and we should test this hypothesis."

"Sounds good. It will take a while to get this set up and we can have a few more discussions on how the idea pans out. In the meantime, we have enough right now to get busy," Kriti smiled.

"Great," said Subodh. "I would take it a step forward and say that we figure out one city and then repeat the same process city by city."

Kriti was nodding in agreement. "I like that. Let's validate the model first and then replicate."

As they walked back after their break, the team knew they were onto something good—something that would uniquely position them in the market and that could direct their future endeavours.

"This is a good process, Javed," said Ankit. "We now have a lot more clarity than we had earlier."

"That's good," said Javed. "Now, what will you not do?"

"For a start, let's stop spending on online advertising and buying shelf space in fancy shops. Medical devices don't need that. We are also spending too much time and money in collaborations with other companies to build alternate sales channels. Let's just focus on our own."

Javed had been busy writing up everything. "Congratulations," he said. "You now have your Vision, a Mission and a Core Strategy."

Strategic Direction: Where Are You Going?

Mission	Vision
We alert to prevent medical emergencies	Ten million active Livewell devices in 5 years

Core Strategy

Customer	Premise
Men and Women between 40 and 55 with a largely sedentary lifestyle.	
General Physicians and other doctors interested in monitoring the health of their patients.	Both GPs and users are interested in keeping users healthy, with longer lives
Owners of other sensors and wearables that could help monitor health (to explore)	
Proposition: A stylish wearable that helps track health-related activities, and connects patients with their doctors; preventing 80% of medical emergencies	
Provisioning: Value Chain • Doctors should be able to set notifications based on some or a combination of sensor readings. • Sensors should be modular so individuals and their doctors can choose the parameters to monitor. • Doctors should have ready access to wearables and training so they can show it to their customers. Should ideally be on display in doctor offices.	
Penetration: Growth	**Perimeter:** Will not do
Market Penetration: City by City. First sign up doctors and get them trained to use the platform. Use doctors in any promotion to end-users.	• No sensors without a medical or health benefit. • No presence in stores that are not medical

The team spent a few minutes looking at the slide Javed had put up. "I like it," said Subodh. "It pretty much sums up all our discussions and clearly states our purpose, what we want to achieve and broadly how we will achieve it."

There were nods around the table. "Great work, all. Now all we must do is detail it and implement it," said Subodh wryly.

"Yes, we do, and I have some recommendations on how to go about it," said Javed. "Let's take a break and get back to it after a few weeks."

SECTION 2
Breakthrough Initiatives: Getting the Big Things Right

The Main Thing is to keep
the Main Thing the Main Thing.

– Stephen Covey

Prologue: Getting the Big Things Right

As agreed, Ankit, Subodh, Kamini and Kriti met with Javed to take stock of the impact of the exercise after four weeks.

"It has been an interesting period," Ankit said. "We started with rolling out the Vision and Mission. The communication exercise went well. There were lively discussions, with some people questioning the Vision and Mission, and others from the team defending them. Just the reactions of everyone were interesting to watch. Subodh and I were spectators after the initial presentation, with employees asking questions and others answering. I also liked that the Mission Statement came up in two management meetings."

"We used the first couple of weeks while we were rolling out our Vision and Mission to work out the implications of our new Core Strategy. The implementation of our Core Strategy touches every part of the business. The technology team is changing their roadmap to get the new customization features in place. The product team is working out the new SKUs and the production system we need to assemble wearables. The marketing team is switching their focus from end-users to doctors. We have yet to figure out how to get the doctors trained in using the new platform," said Subodh.

"But if I am to be totally honest," said Ankit, "all this is happening because Subodh and I are involved with everything. While it is exciting, it is also exhausting. Most of the time it's like we are playing whack-a-mole. Each time we focus on one aspect of our business, something goes wrong in another. Javed, this is a good time to pull another rabbit out of your hat."

Javed smiled. "Right," he said. "We have completed only one of our four levers. Now that we have a good idea of our Core Strategy, we need to focus on what we need to do *now*. You have your Big Hairy Audacious Goal. But what does that mean today? If we don't have clear things to work on, we will struggle to reach our Vision. We need short-term goals that will get us to meet our long-term Vision. Are you familiar with the adage: How do you eat an elephant?"

"Piece by piece," Kamini said.

Javed smiled, "Precisely. We need to break down the impact of changes to the Core Strategy into smaller parts, select the more important of them and then have programs to address each important area. You can then assign those programs to different members team to run."

Kriti nodded her agreement. "Even with clear direction, there will some things you need to prioritize and execute differently. There are only so many things you can do well."

Javed added, "You have your high-level answers to why, what, and how. These are long-term answers. You now need to know what to focus on today—your immediate what's and how's."

Subodh nodded, "OK, that makes sense. How exactly do we go about it?"

"Let's get back to our four levers," said Javed. He put up the picture.

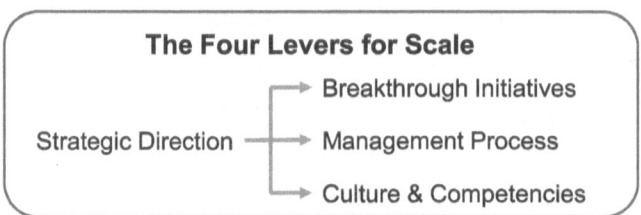

"We have addressed the first part," Javed added. "Which do you think applies to you now?"

"Given the discussion we were just having, it seems like we need to address our Breakthrough Initiatives now," said Kamini. Others nodded.

"That makes sense," said Javed. "Here is the expansion of the second leg."

Lever 2. Breakthrough Initiatives

"We start with our Vision and identify objectives to focus on in the near term," said Javed. "We then put the measures of these objectives on a timeline, so we can see their impact in reaching our Vision. This is effectively breaking up the big 'what' into smaller 'what's'."

"How many objectives should there be?" asked Kamini.

"Having fewer objectives is better for focus," said Javed, "but usually there are between three and five Breakthrough Objectives.

Once we have set our objectives, we identify programs to meet these objectives. Programs are initiatives taken by the company in project mode. There can be several programs for each objective."

"If we have multiple programs being done at the same time, won't it need a lot of time, money and resources?" asked Ankit.

"That is certainly true, but we will stop all other initiatives. At any time, there are many programs of different priorities within a company. Typically, focusing all the available resources will make this less expensive than you think," said Javed. "It will take time however, and that is always in short supply. Part of the process we will follow is to select initiatives that we know are doable, from the considerations of both time and money."

Ankit and Subodh nodded their agreement.

They all finalized the date for the next meeting.

Setting the Right Objectives

In the previous chapters, we talked about the Vision—the Big Hairy Audacious Goal. Objectives are measurable mini-goals; they are checkposts on the way to the Vision.

Objectives are set at every level of an organization.

- A sales organization can have an objective to "Increase revenues to Rs. 30 crores"
- An HR department can have an objective to "Fill every job vacancy within 20 days"
- An individual programmer may have an objective to "Release code for the module on user registration for testing by 30 June"

An objective is written in the form of a 'strong verb, single direct object', and it must be accompanied by a result.

Taken together, objectives with their results are characterized by the acronym SMART. They must be **S**pecific, **M**easurable, **A**chievable, **R**elevant and **T**ime-bound. To understand this better, let us look at an example, in this case the annual appraisals of employees.

> *Objectives are measurable goals that help meet your Vision. They are S.M.A.R.T and are written in the form of a 'strong verb, single direct object'.*

If this objective is written as "Complete all employee evaluations quickly," it does not meet all the criteria. The first part of the sentence is fine. "Complete employee evaluations" meets the criteria of the form of the objective—it starts with a verb and has a single direct object.

However, it is not SMART. It is Specific, in that it is about 'employee evaluation'. It is measurable since 'all' evaluations must be done. It is achievable since it is an annual exercise and has been getting done in the past. Let us assume it's relevant. But it is not time-bound.

Changing the statement to "Complete all employee evaluations by the end of this month" makes it SMART.

In this chapter, we will look at how to come up with objectives that will help you get to your Vision. In a later chapter (Setting Goals across the Organization), we will look at how to extend your company objectives to the entire organization.

Objectives with Results

Let us look at another example of an objective with its result

- "Reduce time to resolve customer complaints to two hours by September 15."

While it is not essential, it is often a good idea to put in the base value of the measure and the base date as well. This improves the communicability of the objective. In the example given earlier, that would translate to "Reduce time to resolve customer complaints from three hours as of March 31, to two hours by September 15."

Another way of writing an objective with its result is to separate all the parts of an objective so you are always sure you have not missed anything. There are five parts to specify:

1. The statement, comprising a strong verb, followed by a single direct object
2. The measure
3. The target value
4. The due date
5. The base value and date (optional).

We can put this in a columnar format. For example, we could represent the objective and its result as the following:

Objective Statement	Measure	Value	Due Date	Base Value
Reduce time to resolve customer complaints	Hours to resolve	2 hours	Sept 15, 20xx	3 hours as on Mar 31, 20xx

Now that we know what an objective is, we will focus on the Breakthrough Objectives that will help scale your organization.

Breakthrough Objectives

Breakthrough Objectives can only be achieved with significant changes in the way the company operates. The target value is usually significantly higher than the base value and is more aggressive than previously achieved.

Breakthrough Objectives focus the energy of an organization into a few goals where extraordinary results are required to achieve the company's Vision.

> *Breakthrough Objectives are set to focus organization energy into a few goals that target extraordinary results to help achieve your Vision.*

Here are some examples:

1. Expand brand presence to 50 districts (from 15 districts) in two years. The company had taken five years to get to 15 districts.
2. Improve customer retention to 90% from 73% in one year. The company had to completely change its service delivery model to achieve this.
3. Bring down personnel turnover below 20% from 35% in one year. This goal was set in the backdrop of average industry personnel turnover of more than 70%.

As you can see, the structure of a Breakthrough Objective is the same as any other objective. They are breakthrough in the sense that the goals set are vital to meeting the Vision and cannot be achieved by doing business as usual.

Quantifying the Vision

Before selecting Breakthrough Objectives, it is important to quantify the Vision into annual targets. This is easier if the Vision is a BHAG since it is already quantified. But even if the Vision is not a BHAG, it is usually possible to put numbers to what achieving the Vision is likely to mean in five years.

Let us consider the Vision Statement of a start-up gaming company. Their Vision was "one million subscribed gamers in five years." They identified what it would mean to reach this goal by year.

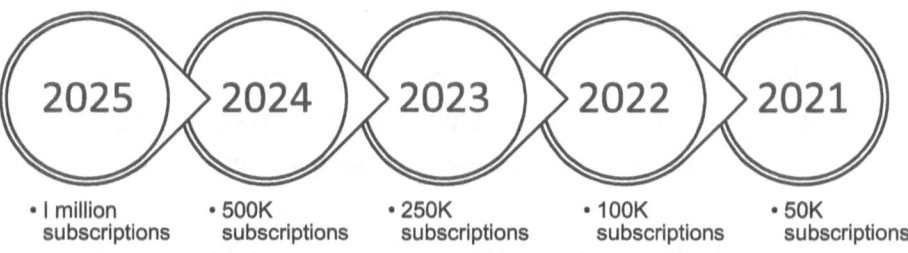

As you can see, the gaming company is planning to double or more than double the number of paid subscribers every year for five years, to reach its target. In the very first year, this translated to 50,000 subscribers.

Once annual numbers are locked down, you can set your Breakthrough Objectives.

Selecting Objectives for Breakthroughs

The purpose of setting Breakthrough Objectives is to bring sharp focus and resources to a few goals that help move your business beyond its regular operations and closer to your Vision.

Occasionally, the company may need to focus more on present issues that may be critical. There could be significant market or environmental changes. For example, the spread of the coronavirus impacted a lot of business activity in 2020. In such cases, there is still clear benefit in bringing focus through a few objectives. However, such factors can result in putting your Vision in abeyance and focusing on present challenges.

Let us continue the assumption that this is not a year with such challenges. There are a few guidelines to selecting the right objectives for breakthroughs:

1. There should not be more than five Breakthrough Objectives at a time (the range is three–five). One of them could be the Vision measure itself.
2. Most objectives should contribute directly to achieving the Vision. These could be market expansion, revenue productivity, larger share of customer wallet, new products or other similar areas.
3. Other objectives may contribute in removing significant hurdles in achieving the Vision. These could be customer satisfaction, product quality, delivery time, system delays, people skills or other similar aspects.
4. Retain a long-term focus. Some of your Breakthrough Objectives should prepare the ground for achieving your longer-term Vision.
5. The objectives should have targets that are aggressive. Meeting them will often require significant additional resources.
6. Together, the objectives should involve the work of a large part of the organization. For example, if a major goal is to do add an acquisition, it may not show up as a Breakthrough Objective.
7. They should not be directly connected. If you have two directly connected measures that are important, pick only one of them, since most initiatives for one will impact the other.

Your objectives should be aligned to your Core Strategy. Once you have identified your objectives, check to make sure that they are aligned.

Let us continue with the example from our gaming start-up. In their strategy session, they decided that they would be distinctive in the number of new products and releases they had as compared to similar competitors. They also decided that their primary source of customer feedback would be from reviewers, and they would increase their relationship with them.

Based on their Vision and Core Strategies, they selected three Breakthrough Objectives for the year.

Objective Statement	Measure	Value	Due Date	Base Value
Increase subscriptions	Number of subscribers	25000	Mar 31, 20xx	12063 as of Mar 31, 20yy
Reduce cost per download	Cost/download	Rs 3	Mar 31, 20xx	Rs 6 as on Mar 31, 20yy
Increase new releases (product or upgrade)	Number of releases/month	8	Mar 31, 20xx	3 as on Mar 31, 20yy

The first objective was to increase subscriptions. This is their primary objective, with their measure being derived directly from their Vision.

The second was to reduce the cost per download. Given their cash constraints, this is an important goal. Since paid downloads alone cannot ever be this low, they needed to focus on organic ways to increase downloads.

The third one was to increase the number of new releases dramatically every month. This reflects their Core Strategy and one that will help them in future years as well.

Let us see how the selected objectives meet all the criteria:

1. Number of objectives should be between three and five. The number here is three.
2. Should contribute directly to the Vision. Both increased subscriptions and increased releases directly contribute to the Vision.

3. Reducing the cost per download mitigates an important constraint in reaching the Vision.
4. The measures should be for beyond the year. Increasing new releases builds capability that will help reach next year's targets.
5. All measures have values that are far more than their usual growth. Both the speed of new releases and the cost/download target cannot be achieved without significant additional resources and focus.
6. The digital marketing and technology development teams together account for 90% of the employees of the company. Hence meeting the objectives will involve most of the people in the company.
7. None of the measures are directly connected.

Defining Your Breakthrough Objectives and Results

Defining company objectives is the responsibility of the CEO. Usually, the CEO will bring together several of their top executives and have a discussion around the direction of the company and the need to either make or change their objectives. This will result in a draft of company objectives with key results.

In a later chapter (Making Choices: The Strategy Matrix), we will discuss the best way to finalize the draft and take the objectives forward to the step of implementation.

Strategic Programs for Your Objectives

Setting Breakthrough Objectives is a key step to meeting your Vision. But having them will not make them come true. To achieve breakthrough results, there are two important tools in your arsenal: first, you need to channel the power of the entire organization (we will deal with that in subsequent chapters); second, the company must invest in a few key initiatives that will propel the company to the next level. These are your Strategic Programs.

> *Strategic Programs are key initiatives that together help meet your breakthrough objectives.*

In the 1990s, Airtel set an objective for profitable growth, and took on the initiative of outsourcing all non-core activities. A primary objective was to ensure that their growth would not lead to a decrease in EBITDA. To achieve that, they tied in their outsourcing contracts to their revenue. For example, they outsourced their customer support and paid their vendors a percentage of the revenue from these customers. This resulted in vendors being fully aligned to Airtel's goal. For many years thereafter, their EBITDA percentage stayed in the twenties, and their market capitalization was the envy of most companies.

Let us look at another example. In the mid-1980s, NIIT decided to double the number of students they trained every year for five years. A part of that would come from existing centres, which were currently growing between 30% and 50% every year. But to double it, they would need a completely different approach. NIIT decided to franchise its centres to take advantage of local entrepreneurial talent. The idea was novel at that time—it was a Strategic Program that had substantial resources allocated to it. The centres also needed to continue to grow simultaneously, and focus had to remain there as well.

If Breakthrough Objectives are set well, they will force team members to think outside the box. A division within a B2B technology company was tasked with increasing B2B user licenses from just 25 in their first year, to 300,000 in five years. Even after much soul searching and many ideation sessions, they were not able to see the number crossing 30,000, a tenth of the goal. Then a team member suggested they consider a revenue source from their customers' customers (a B2B2B option) with a different product variant and pricing policy. As they explored this further, 300,000 became a viable goal and they were able to define a program to meet it.

> *If Breakthrough Objectives are set well, they will force team members to think creatively.*

There can be multiple strategic programs for a Breakthrough Objective. For example, if one of your medium-term objectives is to "Increase monthly online channel revenues by three times by December 20xx," and it is now January of the same year, your programs could be:

1. New online marketing program
2. Dedicated app
3. 100 different channels signed up.

While objectives have the form of 'Strong verb, single direct object', programs are defined by their primary output. When identifying programs, use as few words as possible without compromising the meaning. Programs should be executable between three and eighteen months, with most programs lasting between six and nine months.

Identifying Strategic Programs

Once you have your Breakthrough Objectives, you will find that some ideas for Strategic Programs exist within the company and have not been implemented either because of a lack of time or resources or because they were not seen as being important enough. In a few cases, you may find that you need outside input. This can be in the form of a consultant or of your team benchmarking other companies, both within your industry and outside.

Once your objectives have been studied adequately, you can identify your programs in a workshop with the executive team and other key members. Form groups that will address each of the objectives. There should be at least two groups for each objective. Make sure that teams are heterogenous. The details of this process are covered in the next chapter.

The Program Action Plan

Once the programs and owners are selected, the programs need to be implemented. The Program Leader assigned to the program prepares a Program Action Plan.

The table given here is a format that can be used for this purpose. Each of the elements in the format is explained within the format.

Program Title: The title of the program; typically, the final output of the program	
Program Description: The description you provide must capture the details of the program as discussed when the program was being selected.	
Program Leader: The single person assigned to lead the program	

Scope	Deliverables	Team	Start/End Date
You must state the boundaries of the program here. Is it for a product, or geography, or impact a limited set of customers?	Your deliverables include every type of output that this program will deliver. Can be a report, a machine, a new process...	All the others responsible for the project. You do not need to include everyone involved – for example, the people on a manufacturing line may need to run a new product, but that is their job in any case.	Start and end date of the entire program

Hand off criteria (What will be achieved prior to handoff):

Once the program is completed, it needs to be integrated into the regular operations of the company. The hand off criteria should define what should be achieved for the program to be successful and ready for integration.

Measures to be tracked/impacted post handoff:

Once the program is handed over, its ongoing functioning should be tracked either for some time or should become a regular process to be tracked. The measures that need to be tracked are defined here

No	Significant Activities	Who	When
Serial number	Each significant activity should be written on a separate line. There will be many activities in a program.	Person responsible for the specific activity	Date by which it must be completed

Let us apply the template to one of the programs mentioned earlier: the 'New Online Marketing Program'.

Program Title:	New Online Marketing Program
Program Description:	The existing online marketing activities are not giving expected benefits. This program will try one or more different marketing strategies for a single product and perhaps expand it to other products if the experiment is successful. Some ideas to test were influencer marketing, partnership agreements with parent websites, and a referral program.
Program Leader:	Arvind Kumar

Scope	Deliverables	Team	Start/End Date
Only digital marketing for Sarala soap	Marketing handbook	Quresh Ali Sangeeta Nair Kavita Kaur	Apr 20, 2020 to Nov 15, 2020

Hand off criteria (What will be achieved prior to handoff):	
Number of online soap purchase of Sarala soap to go up from 23000 to 50000 units per month.	
Marketing spend per online purchase to reduce from 20% of sale value to 16% of sale value.	
These targets must be met/exceeded for two consecutive months.	
Measures to be tracked/impacted post handoff:	
Measures will be defined for tracking as part of the program. Output measures are already being tracked. Input measures will be discovered during the program.	

No	Significant Activities	Who	When
1	Benchmark 5 companies who have been most successful with digital marketing (at least 2 from another industry)	Quresh	May 20
2	Get presentations made by digital marketing agencies with their approaches	Sangeeta	May 20
3	Present new plan and get approval and budget	Arvind	May 31
4	Select agency and start implementing plan	Arvind	June 10
5	Mid-course progress review with corrections to be implemented	Arvind	August 1
6	Project completion presentation	Arvind	October 1
7	Completion of Marketing Handbook	Kavita	October 15

What is a Good Strategic Program?

A good set of Strategic Programs can move your company towards your Vision. You can set them every six months, though most programs are set once a year. To be effective, your strategic program should have the following attributes:

1. Significantly impact one or more of your Breakthrough Objectives. We will cover this point in detail in the next chapter.
2. A single owner. This should be an employee who is senior enough to bring resources to bear for the program, and for whom this will be considered a significant achievement.
3. A small team (two–five additional people), who will invest a significant part of their time (between 25% and 100%) for the program, and who will also manage any activities involving a larger part of the company. In a few rare cases, the program may need a large dedicated team.
4. A realistic Program Action Plan, with a complete description, clearly specifying what will be done, by whom and by when.
5. A clear and defined review program. This point will be the topic of a later chapter (Reviews and Reporting Systems).

Making Choices: The Strategy Matrix

The process of coming up with objectives and strategies involves making a lot of choices. Setting the right objectives is easier than identifying programs since the lodestar is the Vision. However, selecting a small set of programs that will move the company towards the Vision is not as easy. You will find that team members will have specific agendas and mindsets, that will make it difficult to wear the organization hat and look at what is best for the organization.

The Strategy Matrix links objectives and programs and summarizes all your priorities in a single page. You can develop the matrix in a workshop with the senior management team. These workshops are most effective when their size is somewhere between 12 and 25 persons.

> *The Strategy Matrix links your breakthrough objectives to your strategic programs, and summarizes them in a single page.*

Step 1. Setting Context

You should start by putting up the Mission, Vision and Core Strategy. Take the time to revisit the Core Strategy. Wherever possible, summarize the most recent insights and present the company SWOT.

Allow time for discussion and possible changes, so that the team is aligned.

Step 2. Finalizing the Objectives

You should usually have the Breakthrough Objectives put together before the workshop. Usually the CEO or the head of the unit presents these objectives along with the reason for their selection. The CEO should encourage discussion. Everyone in the team can have a voice, but only the CEO has the vote. Usually one or two (of five) objectives are changed in some way based on inputs from the team.

As mentioned earlier, you should end up with three to five objectives.

Step 3. Listing Possible Programs

Divide the team into the same number of groups as the number of objectives. Groups should be as diverse as possible. Give two objectives to each group. This will mean that each objective is discussed in two groups.

You should get each group to come up with ideas on 'how' the stretch targets can be met. This is a brainstorming session. Always precede the brainstorming session with a few minutes of brainwriting to give everyone a chance to think before discussion. Each group should document all their ideas, and then come up with three–five ideas for each objective that they believe can (if implemented) meet the goal.

Step 4. Building the Shortlist of Programs

Each group presents their programs, giving reasons for their selection and how they expect the program to impact the objective. Once all the programs are presented, you need to select the programs for the shortlist. There are three broad steps:

1. Combine programs with similar ideas.
2. Get people to vote for the programs. Each participant can vote for five programs. You will find that a few programs will get no vote at all. Remove them from consideration.
3. Discuss each program that got a vote. The people who voted for it should say why they did, and others should say why they did not. In the process, some people may want to switch their votes. Encourage that. Eliminate any program that has no votes after the switching.

Typically, at the end of this stage, you will land up with between 10 and 15 programs.

Step 5. Building the Strategy Matrix

The Strategy Matrix is a way to display correlations between Objectives and Strategies. The diagram given here shows the format:

	Progrm 1	Program 2	Program 3	Program n	Measure	Target	By when
Objective 1	◉	○	◉		Measure 1	Target 1	Date 1
Objective 2		○	◉	◉	Measure 2	Target 2	Date 2
Objective n		△			Measure n	Target n	Date n
Person Responsible	Name A	Name B	Name C	Name N			
Due Date	Date A	Date B	Date C	Date N			
Score	4	5	8	4			

The objectives are set up as rows and the programs as columns.

- The double circles indicate high correlation, indicating that the program has a high impact to the objective.
- The single circles indicate moderate correlation.
- Triangles indicate low correlation.
- A blank square indicates no correlation.

The score is calculated giving a weightage of 4 for each double circle, 2 for each single circle, and 1 for a triangle.

Once you have the scores for each program, look at the ones with low scores and no double circle. Discuss this with the team to decide whether to retain it. Eliminate any that do not have enough contribution to objectives.

Then have the groups discuss whether the company can implement all these programs together—from the perspective of having both good people available and financial resources to support it. The CEO will play the most important role here. Eliminate any program that seem unimplementable.

During the elimination, remember that each objective must have at least one strategic program with a double circle.

Assign a program leader for each program. In most cases, program leaders are assigned from the participants of the workshop.

When the exercise is complete, you should have between 7 and 11 Strategic Programs.

What Makes a Good Strategy Matrix?

Your Strategy Matrix must reflect the key programs of the company. When evaluating your Strategy Matrix, you should check on the following:

1. You should not have more than five objectives and 11 programs. A preferred number is three objectives and eight programs. Anything more than that usually results in loss of focus.
2. Every objective must have at least one program with a double circle. If you do not have one, it is likely that you need to either re-examine whether the objective is important enough or revisit some of the discarded programs to see if one of those should substitute an existing one.
3. Each of your programs must have at least one double circle. Else, while it may be important, it is not key to the objectives and you should re-examine it.

4. You should review the programs having low scores. It is possible that there could be a better one. However, if it has a double circle with one objective and no correlations with others, you should retain it.
5. You should not assign the same person to lead multiple programs.
6. The program leader or program sponsor must be one of the participants of the workshops. Pushing program leadership down the organization hierarchy usually diminishes the importance and likely success of a program.

Once you have completed the matrix, the final step is to revalidate this against the Vision, the SWOT and any other tools that you have used to reach the matrix. You need to ask a few questions:

1. Do the set of programs together move you towards your Vision?
2. Do they leverage your strengths and use the opportunities identified?
3. Do the programs encompass areas identified, or concerns that the team had while debating on the tools?

Whenever you find any dissonance, re-examine the process you went through. Encourage discussions on whether something needs to be changed. Avoid the temptation to add more programs. Instead, ask the participants to substitute an existing program with another one. You may find that one or two programs are replaced through the process.

If you have followed the process diligently, you will find that the entire team is fully onboard with the priorities that have been set and will accept that this is required at the company level. A few may want to further build this for their teams—which is also a good idea. The process is better with a strong external facilitator who understands the business and industry but is not part of it.

Using the Strategy Matrix

The Strategy Matrix is usually drawn up during the annual planning exercise. Many programs take a few months to implement and for results to be seen, so an annual cycle is appropriate.

However external circumstances can result in major changes to both the Core Strategy and the Breakthrough Initiatives. In the first six months of the Covid-19 pandemic, a company providing curriculum solutions to schools changed their objectives and programs twice within four months to plan for the changing market conditions. In a time of rapid change, the Strategy Matrix serves to consolidate thinking, change priorities and communicate those priorities.

> *Whenever you need respond quickly to changes, the Strategy Matrix help to consolidate thinking, change priorities and communicate those priorities.*

Do remember that every selected program must have an accompanying Program Action Plan. The action plan was described in the chapter 'Strategic Programs for your Objectives'.

Getting the Big Things Right: Epilogue

Javed had met Ankit and Subodh and had a discussion on their objectives before their follow-up meeting.

On Javed's suggestion, for this meeting, Ankit had asked the senior management team to join them. That meeting was scheduled for 10 am. The four of them met first at 9am.

As they started the meeting, Javed summarized for Kriti and Kamini. "Ankit, Subodh and I have already spent some time coming up with our key objectives and results."

"So how many objectives are we looking at here?" Kriti asked.

"You will remember that Javed said there should be between three and five objectives. We had our first meeting between the three of us and then Subodh and I came up with our objectives. We have three," said Ankit, while putting up the objectives.

1. Increase the number of doctors in the network from 50 to 2,000
2. Increase sales of Livewell Flex to 5,000 units from 0
3. Reduce turnover in our sales team from 35% to 20%

"Based on our new strategy, we must increase the number of doctors in the network. Since we are targeting only two cities, we have set a target of 25% of all general practitioners in these two cities.

Livewell Flex is our new design where you can plug in different sensor modules. Besides the essential ones, we are providing for an additional five sensors, which can be attached or exchanged. It is still in beta, but we hope to be able to sell 5,000 in the next twelve months.

Finally, we added an objective for salesperson retention. We are not doing well at present, and we will be hiring many more to get to the number of doctors we need. If our salespeople turnover does not come down, we will not be able to get enough doctors on board."

Javed stood up and clapped. "This is tremendous! It's an extremely mature set of objectives and your thinking in arriving at it is excellent."

"It's interesting to me that there are no financial objectives," said Kriti. "When you put these goals up, I was going to recommend you add some financial goals, but now I feel that if we can meet these goals, revenue will follow."

Kamini loved them. "I especially liked your focus on salespeople retention. I think as the organization grows, our people must be looked after, and this is a good start."

"Let's put our goals into a tabular format," said Javed. "so that we are sure that we have captured all the elements required for each objective and their results."

Objective Statement	Measure	Value	Due Date	Base Value
Increase number of active devices	Number of Active Users	1M	Mar-31	502K
Increase sales of Livewell Flex	Number of units sold	5000	Mar-31	0
Reduce turnover of sales team	% Annual Sales turnover	20%	Mar-31	35%

"This is a good set of Breakthrough Objectives. And now I understand you want me and Kamini to leave," Kriti smiled.

"We would be happy to have you, but we are now going to get into the weeds of defining our improvement programs. You may not want to participate," said Ankit. He looked a bit embarrassed after Kriti's statement.

"She was just joking, Ankit," said Kamini. "We are happy to leave you to the weeds."

After Kamini and Kriti left, Javed, Ankit and Subodh joined the management team. Ankit first took them through the entire process till then. There were a few presentations made about the market, the present state of the company and customer feedback. These were made by some of the managers who had been assigned this responsibility. Ankit then presented the Vision, Mission, Core Strategies and Breakthrough Objectives.

Javed then took over. "The objectives you see here show 'what' we want to achieve this year. As you can see, these objectives are challenging. Our exercise today is to come up with the programs we need to meet these objectives. Do not think about constraints while you are doing this. Assume that you will get the people and money needed. We will worry about constraints later."

Over the next few hours, the group worked in teams to identify programs that could support the objectives. Everyone had ideas, and after a few hours there was a list of 38 programs.

"These are too many," said Javed. "Thirty-eight is not focused. We need to select perhaps eight to ten of these to work on."

One of the managers had a point, "If we reduce these programs, then we are unlikely to reach the objectives. So, should we be looking at reducing the objectives?"

Javed explained that not all programs have equal impact. "We need to select the few that will make the most difference."

Javed then facilitated a selection process. By the time it was done, everyone agreed that these programs would together meet their objectives. They then assigned a person to each program and put down the expected date of completion of the program.

MISSION: To help prevent health related problems VISION: 10 million active Livewell devices in 5 years	Enhance Doctor app	Create a doctor kit	Develop Livewell Flex	Launch Livewell Flex	Set up new sales incentive program	Roll out coaching program for salespeople	Measure	Target	By when
Expand the doctor network	●	○	●		○		Number of Doctors	2000	Mar-31
Increase sales of Livewell Flex		○	●	●	△		Number of units sold	5000	Mar-31
Reduce turnover of sales team		△			●	●	% Annual Sales turnover	20%	Mar-31
Person Responsible	Ankit	Sonali	Varsha	Julius	Vinay	Rajshri	CUSTOMER: 1. Men and Women between 40 and 55 with a largely sedentary lifestyle 2. General practitioners (Doctors)		
Due Date	15-Oct	15-Aug	31-Aug	15-Aug	31-Jul	15-Jul			
Score	4	5	8	4	7	6			

"The objectives are shown as rows and the programs are shown as columns," said Javed. "The visuals in the middle show the extent that each program supports an objective. A double circle indicates high correlation, a single circle moderate correlation and a triangle low correlation. As you can see, we have put the name of the leader of each program and the end date by which it is meant to be completed.

Every objective must have at least one program that highly correlates—which we have. We give a weightage of 4, 2 and 1 for each visual and compute the score. Since we have three objectives, any score of 5 or higher indicates that they are each important."

"I like the way it all comes together," said Julian from the marketing function. "I can really relate to the entire matrix, not just to my program. I also like that it is on a single page and everyone can see our priorities for the year."

Ankit added, "I do believe we have narrowed it down to our most important initiatives. I was thinking about my earlier discomfort with having to make this big change happen. Now that we have narrowed it down to a few defined programs and leaders, there is a feeling of both relief and energy to take this forward."

"I like the clarity too," said Subodh, "I am guessing the programs will now have to be fleshed out and reviewed regularly."

"Yes, that's right," said Javed. "I will work with the program leaders over the next few days to complete program plans. Subodh will be chairing the reviews; we plan to do them once a month."

SECTION 3
The Management Process: Aligning the Organization

It's hard, when you are up to your armpits in alligators, to remember that you came to clean out the swamp

– Ronald Reagan

Prologue: Aligning the Organization

Two months after developing the Strategy Matrix, the team met up again along with Javed.

"How is it going?" Javed got to the point right away.

"It's been good," said Ankit. "We have started on all the programs and seem to be progressing well. The program leads have risen to the challenge, and we have been making good progress on two of our Breakthrough Objectives. We may have a challenge with getting our salesperson turnover to below 20%. We are making progress, but it is slow."

"Now that the programs are visible within the organization, others want to participate. I've been telling folks that we need to get these completed first. But it would be nice to engage with the entire company on this," said Subodh.

"It's interesting to hear both your perspectives," said Javed. "Let me put up the four levers again.

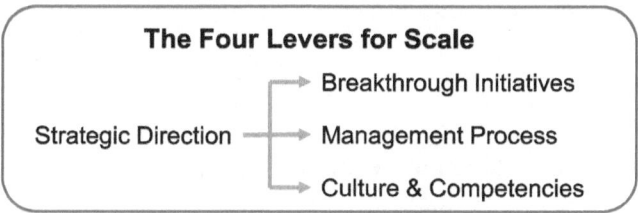

Ankit, one of the most powerful ways to improve retention is to actively focus on the culture of the company. If your salespeople feel they belong, they will stay longer. We could focus on that.

On the other hand, Subodh, instituting a strong Management Process can ensure that every employee and team engages with the priorities of the company."

"Well, why not do both together?" asked Kamini.

"It's possible, but both will need a fair amount of commitment from Ankit and Subodh at the start of the process. It would be better if we prioritized them."

"While I agree that both are important," Ankit said, "I think we should focus on the management system. Our culture is not too bad at present and aligning our new strategy with all teams in Livewell will need all the help it can get." Subodh was nodding, as were Kamini and Kriti.

"My take on the company culture," said Kriti, "is that it is vital in the long-run. But I do believe that a good management system helps with aligning everyone working in Livewell with our Vision and Strategy, and that is more important right now."

"Right," said Javed. "Let me expand the diagram to include the elements here."

Lever 3. The Management Process

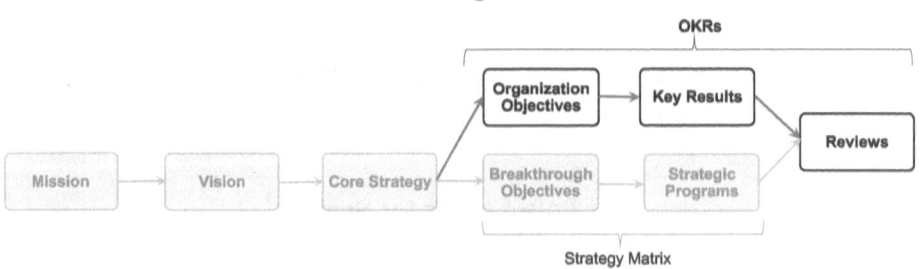

"This is a nice trick you are using Javed," Kamini said, smiling. "Your diagram is complex, but since you are feeding it to us a little bit at a time, we are staying with it, instead of giving up on it. You are feeding us the elephant piece by piece."

Javed smiled back.

"I have a question," Ankit said. "It seems to be that we are adding an unnecessary step. There is a clean flow from our Mission to our Strategy Matrix, where we have identified our priority objectives. Why not go from there? Why are we adding more objectives? As our priorities change, we can always update our Strategy Matrix."

"Good point," said Javed. "What we have done so far is to bring clarity and focus to the objectives and programs that will take us to the next level. That will take a disproportionate amount of time for some people in Livewell. But there are a whole set of important activities that must continue. Your supply chain must continually improve. Your salespeople need to meet their numbers. And so on across Livewell."

"OK, I think I am getting it," said Ankit. "The Management Process helps run all functions of the company. Hence, we need objectives that cover all functions and operations within Livewell. That makes sense. How do we come up with Organization Objectives?"

"The first step is to have a measurement system that covers all key aspects of Livewell. We will use a tool called the Balanced Scorecard. The Balanced Scorecard provides a measurement map based on your Core Strategy. It starts with financial measures, then customer measures, followed by internal process measures and people measures. It shows the linkages between them, so that everyone understands which measure contributes to the other and hence how they contribute," said Javed. "Organization objectives are then easily set from this measurement framework."

"I like the way the four areas seem to link up. For the company to get good financial results, it's important to deliver value to customers. You need internal processes to deliver this value, and your people run those," said Kamini.

"That's exactly right," said Javed.

"The part I don't quite understand," said Ankit, "is that these measures will somehow be linked to our Core Strategy. I can understand that it can be linked to our industry or our kind of business, but won't everyone have the same measures?"

"That's an excellent question," said Javed. "The scorecard is a prioritized set of measures, not a complete set. The prioritization is done based on a number of factors: your industry, whether you are growing or stable and your Core Strategy, among others."

Ankit looked doubtful. "That sounds too good to be true. We have many processes and measures. It seems like it will be complex. I am going to have to trust you on this one, Javed. If it's possible, we should certainly do it. I am happy to try."

Javed smiled. "I am not done yet. Once you have the measurement system in place, you need to be able to use those measures to set team and individual goals. A method that many companies use today is called 'Objectives and Key Results' or OKR. It's a transparent system of short-term goals and results for teams and individuals."

"Now you are confusing me," said Kamini. "I understood that the Balanced Scorecard will help define all the measures we need, along with their linkages. We can then use these to set objectives for the company. Then you brought in another system called OKR. I did not understand the need for it at all."

Kriti said, "Javed, let me try explaining this, so I am also clear that I have understood. Kamini, you are right about using the Balanced Scorecard to define all the measures. We will use it to set up our measurement framework. Once we have the framework in place, we will follow the OKR process to actually define the objectives."

Kamini said, "I think I get it now. Also, I just searched for OKRs on my phone and it seems that Google, LinkedIn and Twitter along with many other tech companies are using it today. It must be a good thing."

Javed continued, "Thanks, Kamini and Kriti for clearing that up. In the OKR system, every team and individual decide their own OKRs. Usually that includes three—five objectives and around three measures or Key Results for each objective."

"Are you saying that individuals will decide their own OKRs?" Subodh was surprised. "Will that not mean that people will pull in all directions?"

"Well, the way you will implement it is to make the entire system visible to everyone," continued Javed. "The company OKRs will be done first, so that everyone knows what you are trying to achieve. Employees will have a few fixed OKRs, but they can take on others that will help them meet company goals or in some cases personal goals like acquiring a new skill. And the entire company will do this exercise every quarter."

"I don't know about that," said Subodh. "I love the first part of what you said. I think a transparent system is great, and I can see our employees loving the ability to select some of their own goals. But doing this every quarter? It seems like a lot of work. Our current budgeting and appraisal process is done annually and it's a painful process. To set goals every quarter seems like a lot of work."

"Annual goal-setting is too slow for a tech start-up, and from what Kamini just mentioned, even very large companies are finding that they need the flexibility to alter direction every quarter," said Javed. "It is a change, but I think you will find that employees get it within one or two quarters."

"I agree with you, Javed," said Ankit. "Our budgeting and review process does not seem to give us the benefits we want, and we have recast the numbers within the first few months anyway."

Subodh nodded thoughtfully. "Fair enough. I agree that our process was not yielding much. This is worth a try."

Ankit said, "I have a question though? How is this compatible with our Breakthrough Objectives and programs? Are we going to have two separate processes?"

"That's a great question," said Javed. "The Breakthrough Objectives and programs will be integrated into the OKR process. Breakthrough Objectives will show up at the company level and programs will show up in the work that teams are doing. They merge together quite easily."

Javed continued, "The OKR system also recommends a way to do reviews. You will have a weekly review process where individuals and teams self-evaluate. Then they can discuss their progress on the Key Results within the team or the manager. The discussion is usually focussed on helping achieve the results," said Javed.

Subodh was shaking his head. "Javed, you have been to our company and know that we work pretty much seven days a week across all hours. This is just not implementable."

"OK, let me ask you this. How many hours a week do you spend with each of your direct reports discussing what they need to do, helping them prioritize, giving them feedback and directions?" asked Javed.

"Perhaps, two-three hours every week. Why?"

"What if I were to tell you that this kind of interaction can go down to less than an hour if you spend 30 minutes each week on the OKR. And perhaps another two hours a quarter. What the OKR does is organize work for everyone. You will find after a while that when your team does not do what you believe they should be doing, you can help them tweak their OKR and the alignment happens almost magically," said Javed.

Kriti nodded her agreement. "Subodh, Ankit, I realize that Javed is hard selling the OKR. But I can tell you that this sets up your management system and will make your life a lot easier."

Ankit and Subodh looked at each other. "I think we are sold on the idea," said Ankit. "Let's do it."

Measurement

One of the foremost management gurus of our time, Peter Drucker famously said, "If you can't measure it, you can't manage it."

While measures have been around for centuries, their formal use in a management system started sometime in the early twentieth century. Companies began using them as a method of tracking performance. Measures are an integral part of business rhythms today, and they are often used to indicate individual performance as well.

To be an effective management tool, a measure should have a target value and a time by which it should be achieved.

> *A measure should have a target value and a time by which it should be achieved.*

Let us use an example. Say, you have a team of tele-callers. Whenever you walk by them, one of them always seems to be on break or chatting with her co-workers. Her performance is low as well, but not low enough to haul her up to management. You speak to her, but she denies it. If you were tracking the number of calls she made and the duration of each call, this would not be a debate, and you would be able to tell her that she needs to improve.

Measurement is everywhere. It is in the quality of your product, the timeliness of delivery, sales achievement, customer satisfaction, individual performance and financial results. As organizations grow, there is little that is not measured.

Over time, there will be some areas that are measured better than others. In the example of the tele-caller, the measurement can be a manual log or some Customer Relationship Management (CRM) software. If it is a manual log, the measurement would be very tedious and may not be worth the effort.

Lagging and Leading Indicators

There are two types of measures: those that measure outcome and those that measure an input or a process. The first is called a *lagging indicator* and the latter is called a *leading indicator*.

The output measure is a lagging indicator since it measures something that has already happened. Since it has already happened, you can no longer change it. As a measure of performance, it works well, but as a tool for decision-making, the information comes too late to change anything.

An example of this can be sales orders received in a month. It certainly indicates how well the company is doing, but it reflects what has already transpired. It is important to track that, but it is not enough since it does not help you manage for future results.

Lagging indicators show the consequences of your actions. It shows if sales are up or down, production is up or down, or product quality is up or down. Your entire financial system consists of lagging indicators. How much did you spend? Are your profits up? All stakeholders want to know if your business is doing well. As a demonstration of results, lagging indicators are the way to go.

As a crude analogy, imagine you are driving a car and you run over an object on the road and nearly have an accident. The rear-view mirror shows you the object on the road—it is a lagging indicator. What you need however is to pay more attention to what you can see through your windshield and to avoid the object. That is your leading indicator, so you can drive better.

There are always leading indicators that you can work on to ensure that you get to the appropriate lagging indicator. For example, if you have many customers at an advanced stage of discussion, a certain percentage of those will become orders. You can hence use a sales funnel to predict orders.

Leading indicators are more in your control. Did you make enough sales calls? Were all project milestones completed? Did you get the right people hired in time? When you work on your leading indicators, you usually get more predictable results.

Leading indicators are steppingstones towards the lagging indicators. If you want to improve sales, you may want to improve sales productivity. To improve productivity, you may want to train your people better and to increase the number of calls they make every day. By focusing on increasing the leading indicator—say calls per day—you will ensure that sales productivity increases, which in turn increases sales.

Selecting the Right Indicators to Measure

What you measure depends on what you want to achieve—your objective. In an earlier chapter, we have discussed how the company's Vision and Strategy lead to its annual objectives.

Let us assume that one of your objectives was the following:

- Increase revenue per tele-caller per month from $15,000 per month to $20,000 per month by the end of the year.

Now, to do that, you may need additional indicators, which will help you reach your objective. The diagram given here shows how these indicators may be linked.

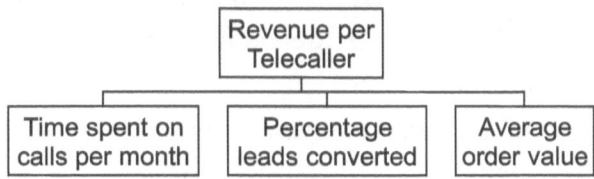

In this example, the revenue per tele-caller has three leading indicators

1. The time spent on calls per month: This is about the efficiency of the tele-caller, and it tracks how much activity the person is doing.

2. Percentage of leads converted: This is about effectiveness, and it reflects the skill of the tele-caller.
3. Average order value: This is usually about the product mix. This may be a constant if your tele-caller is selling a single product with a standard discount, or it may be a measure of product saleability if the tele-caller has a portfolio of products.

Now, if your task were to improve tele-caller revenue, the second indicator is a function of the tele-caller's skill level. If your company keeps track of tele-caller training, it would be a particularly important element to measure. This will change the diagram to

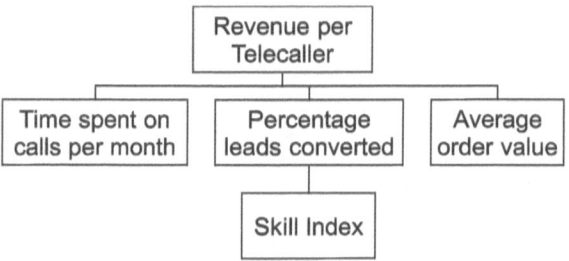

But between them, these indicators may not be enough to improve the tele-caller revenue. Let us consider a few other elements:

1. Customer satisfaction on your product can impact sales productivity. It is much easier to sell a product that customers rate highly. This may be dependent on timeliness of delivery and product quality.
2. The goal of improving revenue per tele-caller is to increase overall revenue. So, the number of tele-callers must be an important measure.
3. It is also likely that the quality of the database being used by the tele-callers will also have a big impact on how effectively leads are converted to sales.

Putting these factors in changes our diagram to the following:

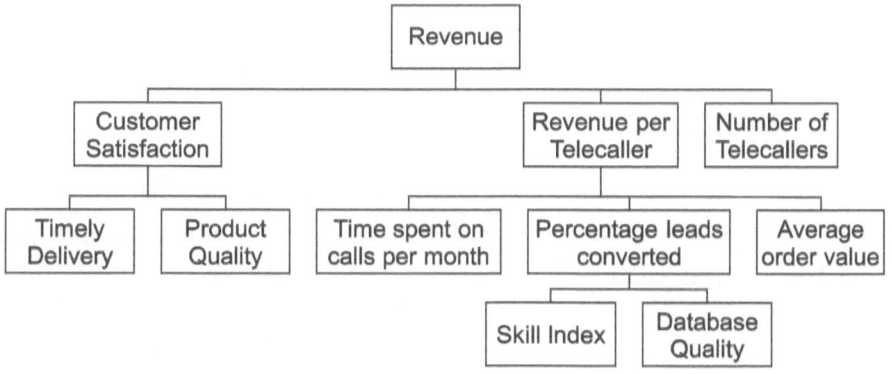

The Balanced Scorecard

At this point, you could very well be asking yourself whether this seems like a never-ending exercise, with new measures surfacing ever so often as a new linkage is discovered. Or even worse, whether the number of measures will keep growing till there are too many to track.

Having a comprehensive framework is important so that systems are in place to allow managers to get the right information and take the right decisions. The BSC is an effective management tool to put together the measurement framework for your company.

In the 1990s, Kaplan and Norton introduced the BSC. Their framework provided a structure for developing Key Measures, by balancing four perspectives of an organization—financial, customer, internal processes, and organizational capacity. Together, these perspectives ensure that all aspects of your company are linked to your company's Vision and Strategic Objectives.

The Scorecard provides a detailed framework for developing indicators. In their book *The Balanced Scorecard*, Kaplan and Norton discuss how companies at different stages should look at different indicators for each of the four perspectives and the linkages between the perspectives. They recommend indicators for specific kinds of objectives.

> *The Balanced Scorecard provides a detailed framework for developing a comprehensive set of indicators for your business.*

Let us take the earlier example that started out for tele-caller productivity but now encompasses other processes in the company. In a BSC framework, the measures would be represented as follows:

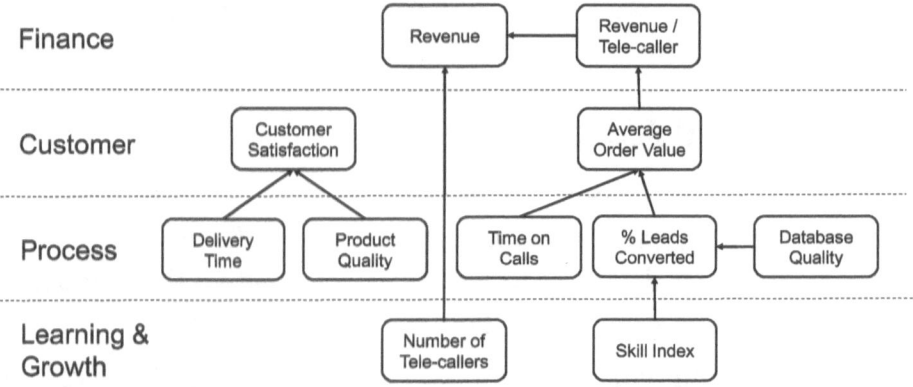

As you can see, the relationships between measures are established, and they are grouped into the four areas. It is immediately apparent that the framework is not complete.

1. The link between Customer Satisfaction and Average Order Value is important, but not significant. Customer Satisfaction is more likely to result in repeat orders, which in turn can lead to increased revenue.

2. The Number of Tele-callers as a measure directly to Revenue seems odd, since it is likely that there would be other sources of revenue. Hence a measure of Order Value from Tele-callers can be another Customer measure, that can in turn connect to Revenue.

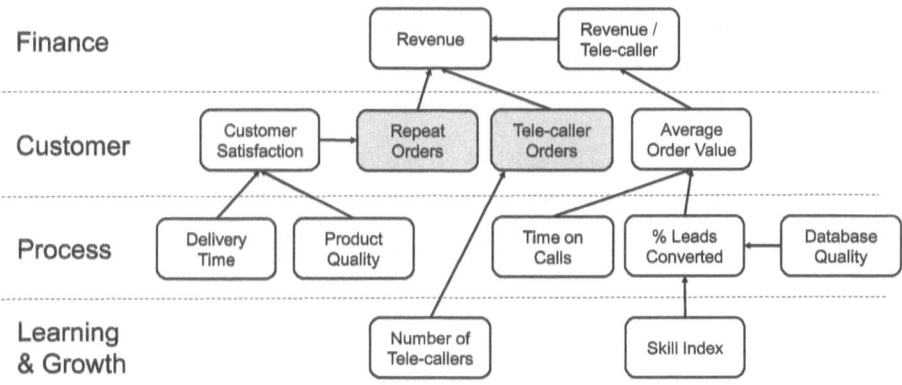

By expanding this process to other functions, you can develop a framework for the entire company. Let us now look at all the types of measures that can be considered for each of the four areas

The Themes within the Balanced Scorecard

These are the possible themes within each area of the BSC. Study these themes to get ideas on the kinds of measures you need to set up. Your company need not have measures from each theme.

Financial: This perspective views organizational financial performance and the use of financial resources. Financial indicators tend to be lagging indicators. The major themes here are as follows:

1. Revenue Growth: To meet this objective, you will have indicators that measure absolute revenue, revenue by market or percentage revenue from products.
2. Cost Reduction: Here you could consider indicators like unit cost, cost/employee or cost/salesperson.
3. Asset Utilization: Here your indicators could be elements like Return on Investment or Return on Capital Employed.

Customer/Stakeholder: This perspective views organizational performance from the point of view of the customer or of other key stakeholders. The major themes here are as follows:

1. Market Share: Indicators here reflect your proportion of business in a market, such as volume market share, revenue market share or number of customers.
2. Customer Acquisition: This can range from a simple count of customers to customers added for a product line or ratios of paid customers to visitors on a website.
3. Customer Retention: This can also be in absolute numbers such as customer churn or relative numbers such as percentage retention over time.
4. Customer Satisfaction: Examples here would include a customer satisfaction index, ratings on your website, number of complaints or on-time delivery.
5. Customer Profitability: Some companies now measure ARPU (average revenue per user) or net profit per customer.

Internal Process: This perspective views organizational performance through the lenses of quality and efficiency. It ties internal functions to customer and business results. The major themes are as follows:

1. Innovation Processes: Research and new product development would be covered under this, with measures such as cycle time for product development or revenue from new products.
2. Operations Processes: All processes involved in developing and delivering your product or service are covered under this. Cycle times, error counts, machine productivity and error costs are usually indicators of these processes.
3. Sales and Marketing Processes: Indicators like channel growth and profitability, lead conversion ratios are considered.
4. After-sales Processes: Measures associated with product repair and post-sales support are covered under this.

Organizational Capacity (originally called Learning and Growth): This perspective views organizational performance through the lenses of human capital, infrastructure, technology, culture and other capacities that are key to superior performance.

1. Employee Processes: These would measure employee retention (usually measured as a percentage of staff turnover), employee satisfaction (typically measured through a survey), and employee productivity (often measured as revenue per employee).
2. Staff Competencies: Indicators here are often training-related, such as numbers of training days/employee, but they can also focus on specific competencies needed.
3. Climate for Action: This covers motivation, empowerment and alignment, and measures employee and team performance.

Developing Your Balanced Scorecard

You can create your own BSC by following these steps:

1. Start with your Vision and Breakthrough Objectives. Define the measures for these, and then come up with the leading indicators for each.
2. Integrate any missing elements of your Core Strategy. Your Breakthrough Objectives will reflect your current priorities, which may not reflect all elements of your Core Strategy. But these must be measured and tracked to retain your competitive advantage.
3. Put these measures within the BSC groups and connect them as appropriate. Wherever there are missing measures, put them as well.
4. Now look at the themes mentioned earlier and carefully consider whether any of these themes can apply to your business at this time. Incorporate them into your BSC.

5. Check for balance. Does one area seem to have very few measures? Consider if you are missing something and add them. This often happens within Learning and Growth.
6. Finally, eliminate. Once you have the set of measures, remove those that do not contribute to any important decision.

For example, applying this to our gaming company, we get the following:

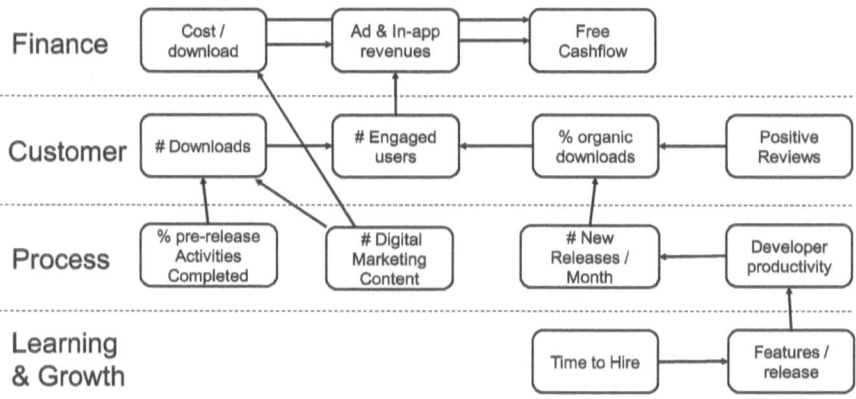

The selected BSC measures reflect the Vision, Breakthrough Objectives and Strategy of the company.

Let us look at a few of their selected measures:

- The only cost measure within the Finance section is Cost/Download. This is not their biggest cost; that would be the salaries. However, it is the element they can control and one that improves their unit profitability.
- They are tracking the number of positive reviews. They could be simply tracking the 'number of reviews', but that would not provide information on the quality of these reviews. However, the 'number of positive reviews' does.
- They need to improve their number of new releases. For that, they need to improve their 'developer productivity' and monitor

the number of 'features in each release'. The important causality here is to be have a short 'time to hire', whenever they have developer attrition.

Company-wide scorecards usually have between 20 and 50 measures. When depicted properly, the BSC provides clear visibility and demonstrates causality. This helps to understand how all the pieces of the strategy link together. It gives employees a way to understand the important elements of their role and how it benefits the company.

Measurement Traps

While measurement is the lifeblood of an organization, there are a few important principles to internalize in setting up measurement systems.

Good Enough 'Is' Good Enough

A company with a time-logging process introduced a new sub-system in which every person attending a meeting would have to log in a meeting ID and meeting type. They were already tracking the time spent on meetings, but now they wanted to see which type of meetings people attended. This information was proudly presented in the next management meeting. The sub-system was removed after the CEO asked what purpose it served.

A company restructured by product category and wanted to assign responsibility of product-wise profitability. Of the 20-odd cost heads that went into each product, 15 of them accounted for less than 10% of costs. Instead of detailing these costs, they were allocated as a percentage of revenue. This would create a possible variation of around 1%, but it was so small that it would not impact any decision.

When setting up a system to capture a measure, it is important to weigh the cost and time of the measurement against its value in decision-making.

> *When setting up a system to capture a measure, it is important to weigh the cost and time of the measurement against its value in decision-making.*

Differentiate between Regular and Periodic Measures

Regular measures are those that should be tracked on an ongoing basis and hence require systems to capture and track them. Periodic measures are needed for one-time decisions. There is additional effort involved in collecting this information, which is fine because it is not required on a regular basis.

Let us go back to the example of the gaming company. In their effort to improve developer productivity, they needed to do two things. First, to make sure that their developers were coding for at least six hours every day. This is a regular measure and there should be a system to report it regularly. Second, to improve the development process. That required deep analysis of a few projects to locate inefficiencies in the process itself. Once it was completed, this data did not need to be tracked regularly.

Do not make the mistake of building systems for measures that will be used infrequently. It is an unnecessary overhead.

> *Do not build systems for measures that will be used infrequently. It is an unnecessary overhead.*

Setting Goals across the Organization

Historically, setting goals has been a top-down process. There are company goals set by top management, which are then passed down to the next lower level, and so on down the organization so that every person knows what they need to do. This process is neat, but unreliable. It is neat because company goals are distributed across the organization and each person knows their goals. It is unreliable because employees do not own their goals.

Over time, the process changed to be bottom-up as well as top-down. At the company level, goals are set that need to be met by lower levels. However, the company sets only a few strategic goals. People down the line are free to contribute to these goals and to have their own goals as well.

The other change over the years has been the speed of change, especially with the increasing use of technology. Goal-setting used to be an annual process, but market dynamics can now change sooner, and companies must react quicker. This often results in the goal-setting process being put aside, with managers taking decisions and changing course mid-stream.

Introducing Objectives and Key Results

Objectives and Key Results (OKRs) were initially used by Andy Grove to lead Intel at the time of intense change and challenge. It was then adopted by several leading technology companies, including Google and Twitter, as the key Management Process by which their company can set targets and monitor results.

An OKR uses multiple Key Results (measures) for a single objective. In this system, the objective is a simple statement—such as Double Sales Orders within six months—and the measures support this objective. The system is usually set up in a quarterly cadence. Objectives often remain the same across quarters, but Key Results will usually be completed within one quarter.

> *Objectives and Key Results (OKRs) combine longer term Objectives with quarterly Key Results.*

In the case of OKRs, Objectives show intent while Key Results show the outcomes. Like Objectives, OKRs are also SMART (**S**pecific, **M**easurable, **A**chievable, **R**elevant and **T**ime-based).

Let us look at an example.

Objective: Double sales orders from previous year.

Key Results for the quarter:

1. Hire 15 new salespeople.
2. Increase number of sales calls per week from 12 to 15.
3. All salespeople must complete two days of training in the new products being launched this quarter.

For them to be effective, OKRs should have some additional attributes:

1. They should be transparent. Once set, all OKRs are visible to anyone within the company.
2. Many companies provide for Key Measures that are either committed or aspirational. Committed OKRs have targets that should be met. Aspirational OKRs are challenging stretch targets that teams and individuals set for themselves. If you find all aspirational results being achieved, they were probably not aspirational enough.
3. OKRs are set for teams as well as individuals. Hence a division will have its own OKRs, and the head of the division and other team members will have personal OKRs. You may want to do it first for the company and senior executives, and only then roll it down to the rest of the company.

> *The real advantage of OKRs is that they provide a viable method for quarterly planning and goal setting, with high engagement and transparency.*

How to Formulate OKRs at the Company Level

We have earlier explained how objectives are decided for a company. Many companies set their company-level objectives once a year but modify them every quarter as needed. There are a few reasons to change objectives every quarter:

1. The pace of change in the industry is so rapid that it is important to revisit company goals every three months.
2. Your company or division is young, and your plans are evolving too fast for an annual planning event to be meaningful.
3. There is a specific opportunity or threat that is important enough to revisit the plan for the year. For example, a competitor may have launched a new product that is making a big impact, and you must counter it.
4. Your business is cyclical and different quarters may require a different focus. For example, if you are in the education business, admissions may be a focus for one quarter, but not for the remaining quarters.

Key Results are the outcomes expected during the quarter. They must be measurable and together must ensure that the objective is met over a period of time. In the earlier example of doubling sales, adding salespeople, increasing calls and providing training on the new product should result in sales orders doubling.

There should typically be between three and five objectives at the company level. We have already discussed how company-level objectives are set. Some objectives may extend over several quarters or even years. Others may be the need of the hour and may only show up for one or two quarters; for example, implementing a new company-wide CRM may be a focus for a single quarter.

Usually the CEO and top executives will meet to decide on the focus for the quarter and agree on the company-level OKRs. Even when objectives remain the same, the key results will change from quarter to quarter.

OKRs for Teams

Each business unit formulates their OKRs. Typically, half to two-thirds of business entity objectives will be aligned directly to that of the company. Entities will have their own priorities in addition to those of the company. For example, HR may want to focus on company-wide training, which is critical to the company but is not identified as a company-level OKR.

Having a well-formulated BSC as a reference point is particularly useful for business entities and teams. They can use the scorecard to understand the relationships between their functions and the company at large and can hence formulate Objectives and Results that support the overall Vision. This allows every level in the organization to contribute their ideas and reflect them in their own Objectives and Key Results.

Entity-level OKRs are also set in the same way as the company-level OKRs, with the management team of the business entity getting together once every quarter to decide these. Some functional objectives may stay the same for many periods, but Key Results will always be set for the next period.

As each level completes their OKRs, they discuss them with their next level. This ensures that the alignment is complete. Often, a few key results are changed because of this discussion.

Individual OKRs

Once business entity-level OKRs are set, individuals can set their OKRs and review them with their managers. Individual OKRs can be aligned to the company, the business entity or even a competency that may be relevant for the company in future. For example, you may have an employee interested in acquiring a new skill or who may want to try out a new product idea. Individuals are often encouraged to have one OKR aligned to the company's Strategic Direction, even when it is not aligned to the current Company Objectives.

It is vital for heads of divisions to have personal OKRs. In some OKR implementations, the manager of a team takes the teams goals as their personal OKRs. That is not the correct method. By setting their own personal OKRs, managers signal that they are part of the process and are prepared to make themselves accountable to their teams. For example, if a team has a revenue target, the manager may take on a personal OKR to meet a certain number of customers during the quarter.

> *Individual OKRs by managers, signal that they are prepared to make themselves accountable to their team.*

Cadence of Measurement

The frequency of goal setting should be based on the nature of the industry and the function of the entity. In a fast-changing industry, and in the case of most start-ups, it is beneficial to set goals every quarter. But even within rapidly changing industries, there are processes that are well established and do not need a new set of key results every quarter. You will find these in mainline functions like product delivery and customer call handling, and in support functions like finance and administration.

Google is often quoted as the benchmark to emulate in OKRs today. OKRs work for them as most of their focus is on data and technology. They also employ a young and mobile workforce, and hence must deal with many brilliant minds who need continuous change. The innovation culture that OKRs support works very well for Google. On the other hand, Amazon has a huge delivery network where execution capability is more important. Amazon does not need the cadence of new objectives every quarter. Typically, more creative processes have changing OKRs and production OKRs remain the same over periods of time.

Converting Objectives to OKRs

Let us assume that our gaming start-up decided to use OKRs with a cadence of three months. We convert one of their objectives into an OKR.

Objective Statement	Measure	Value	Due Date	Base Value
Increase subscriptions	Number of subscribers	25000	Mar 31	12063 as of Mar 31

Objective: Increase subscriptions

Key Results:

1. Number of subscribers to be 16,000 by Jun 30
2. A referral feature to be added to all games by May 15
3. A Spanish version of two games to be released by Jun 15

As you can see, at the company level, the annual result is now for the quarter. Also, there are two specific prioritized activities that should help with increasing subscriptions. The first is a referral feature so that existing subscribed gamers get some benefit in case they can get their friends to join, and the second is to expand to new languages.

Now let us see what the marketing department can do in relation to this objective.

Objective: Increase downloads

Key Results:

1. Increase monthly downloads by 8% every month
2. Sign cross-promotion agreement with two other gaming companies by May 30, 20yy

3. Get at least two games into five top ten games lists by Jun 30, 20yy
4. Improve content to increase click-throughs by 30% by Jun 30, 20yy

Objective: Increase ratio of subscribers to downloads

1. Release AI-based targeted notifications by May 31, 20yy
2. Promote referral feature through in-app adverts. Release on May 16, 20yy
3. Survey 100 recent subscribers and identify actions to take by Apr 30, 20yy

As you can see, the marketing department has two objectives that are aligned to the company objective. As before, all results are set to be completed within the quarter.

How Balanced Scorecards, Breakthrough Objectives, Strategic Programs Link to OKRs

The BSC defines the measurement framework for the company. It ensures balance between financial, customer, process, and learning and growth. Since it reflects all functions of the company, Key Results of managers should address each measure of the BSC. If there are BSC measures that not covered by the Key Results of any manager, it can show an imbalance that should be addressed.

Breakthrough Objectives are a part of the company's objectives for the current period. They are selected based on their impact on the Vision of the company and to provide focus on a few things that will make the most difference. They usually constitute the company-level OKRs.

Strategic Programs become key result areas (and hence OKRs) for the people assigned these programs (including team members). During the period of the program, this is sometimes their only job.

Completing OKRs

There are usually four separate sets of activities to define OKRs:

1. Approximately a month before the end of a quarter, the company releases their OKRs at the company level.
2. Over the next two weeks, all entities and individuals submit their own OKRs.
3. In the next week, the OKRs are aggregated at the company level to see if the company-level OKRs are likely to be met (as a combination of team OKRs). Where there are gaps, specific discussions are held with groups.
4. In the final week, managers have their discussions with the business units reporting to them as well as their direct reports to finalize all OKRs.

On completion of this process, all OKRs are visible to all employees in the company, so anyone who is interested can see not just their own OKRs but also those from the entire organization.

Reviews and Reporting Systems

Once you have your goals in place, as described in the previous chapter, people in your organization will know what they need to achieve individually and how it fits into the goals of the organization.

Reviews ensure that the focus remains on measures and that progress is monitored, so that your company reliably achieves its objectives.

What is a Review?

The term 'review' is used very often within organizations, as in "Let us meet tomorrow to review your program or performance or progress." Often, reviews are used to direct the project and to discuss or even plan the possible next steps. There are quarterly business reviews or QBRs where the status of the company is presented through visual aids to show its progress and to discuss plans with investors or in, the case of a division, with senior management. And finally, there are employee reviews, where an employee is assessed for their performance, which is often linked to compensation and development plans.

Each of these reviews are different, but they should ideally follow the same set of rules. The dictionary definition of the term is "a formal assessment of something with the intention of instituting change if necessary." Let us break this up into its constituent bits.

1. A review is 'formal'; it is prepared by a person or team for another person or team.
2. It is an assessment. For an assessment to be effective, it must be against a plan. You can assess a program or a measure, but there should be a plan to review.

3. The intention is to 'institute change'. The need for this change comes because something is not happening the way it should.
4. The change must be 'necessary'. If during the review, the measures or actions reported are as per plan, no change is necessary.

So, expanding on the definition, let us understand what a review is.

1. It is always against a plan. The plan can be a 'Key Result'—as defined in the previous chapter—steps in a project, a specific outcome or a metric with a target.
2. The presentation must include the following:
   a. The plan and the achievement.
   b. The gap between the plan and the achievement along with the underlying or 'root' cause of that deviation.
   c. Actions that will be taken to meet the goal (if there is a negative deviation).
3. The purpose of a review is to understand the gaps, the root cause and the action plan, to assess whether these are likely to succeed and to recommend changes to the actions or to the plan itself.

This is true for any review, ranging from the QBR to individual appraisals. In effect, a review is a problem-solving exercise.

Now, let us see what a review is not.

1. It is not a planning session. If during a review it becomes evident that a whole new plan is required, that should be done in a separate session.
2. It is not a blame game. The idea is not to assign blame to an individual. That defeats the purpose of a review.
3. It is not a glorified presentation of achievement. While it is important to highlight successes, the focus of the review is to help the entity being reviewed to meet its gaps, if any.

> *An effective review is a problem-solving exercise.*

The OKR system covers both goal-setting and reviews. In this chapter, we will use examples based on OKR goals and Strategic programs. However, if you are using any other system, the principles and ideas here will work for you.

In this chapter we will look at Business Reviews and Program Reviews.

Business Reviews

Every business entity should have a recurring review of its progress against measures. With OKRs, the recommended cadence is weekly.

In any review, there is a reviewer and a reviewee. Let us say the marketing department in a company is being reviewed, and that the marketing department reports to the CEO. In this case, the head of marketing is the reviewee and the CEO is the reviewer. There are many formats for reviews. It is possible that the CEO has the CFO to help him/her and that other business entities are also present who can contribute to the review. On the side of the reviewee, multiple people may make presentations. But for an effective review, there is only one reviewer and one reviewee.

The structure of the review itself usually has three components:

1. The Overview: The overview includes the highlights of the previous period, triumphs, tragedies and other points of interest. At higher levels of the company, this may include trends in the market, competitor activity and any other shifts that can impact the business.
2. Performance: The presentation on performance should be done against a stated plan. The first part is often an update of the progress against actions agreed to in the previous review.

This is followed by business measures that can be OKRs, for example, showing progress against plan. Wherever there is a negative gap (performance is lower than plan), there should be an explanation of the cause and a plan to make up the gap where possible.

3. Plan: The last part of the review involves looking at actions to bridge the gaps and perhaps modifying the target numbers for the next period. Modifying the goals themselves is not recommended. All agreed actions should be consolidated and documented either during or immediately after the review.

Preparing for the Review

For the reviewee, preparation for the review culminates in getting the presentation ready.

Putting Data and Analysis Together for the Completed Period

The first step is to collect the data. In most cases, this data is readily available. For example, if revenue or collections is a Key Result, information on it will be available within the financial system; or if a Key Result is the number of customers added, it will be available from the CRM system. In some cases, it may need to be computed, and in a few cases even estimated—for example, whether a project will complete on time as measured by its percentage completion.

Once the data is available it can be plugged into your review template, so you can see the gaps between the plan and the achievement. You should also update the status of actions agreed on by you. For each measure, quantitative progress should be supported by a qualitative assessment—you can consider using green (if you are on track to achieve the goal), amber (if you are likely to achieve your goal) and red (if you see significant challenges in achieving the goal) to visually highlight your progress.

Let us consider the presentation of the marketing head in our gaming start-up. We will consider one objective. We will assume this review is being done halfway through the quarter, at the end of the sixth week.

Objective: Increase Downloads

Key Result	Quarter Goal	Expected till now	Achieved	Status	Comment
Monthly downloads to increase by 8% every month	600K	340K	360K	Green	On track to exceed goal
Sign cross-promotion agreement with other gaming companies by May 30, 20yy	2	1	1	Amber	3 conversations, not promising
Get at least 2 games into 5 top ten games lists by Jun 30, 20yy	2	1	4	Green	1 more game should get to top 20 this month
Improve content to increase click-throughs by 30% by Jun 30, 20yy	30%	16%	1%	Red	Planned methods not working. New plan enclosed

As a reviewee, you should meet with your team, discuss gaps and their cause or causes, and together come up with an action plan. Where the gaps are large, it is advisable to use formal problem-solving methods. Follow any recognized problem-solving approach, such as those popularized by quality gurus like Deming or Crosby, or newer approaches like 6 Sigma.

Planning for the Next Period

Once you are clear about your gaps and the plans to close them, work out your plans to meet the goals for the next period. Again, this is about being sure that you and your team's actions will meet the goals that you expect to be met.

Key Result	Quarter Goal	Expected by next period	Achieved till now	Goal for next period	Plan for next period	Comment
Monthly downloads to increase by 8% every month	600K	390K	360K	30K	50K	Continuing past trend
Sign cross-promotion agreement with other gaming companies by May 30, 20yy	2	1	1	0	0	Need ideas
Get at least 2 games into 5 top ten games lists by Jun 30, 20yy	2	1	4	0	1	2 games in top 15 in category
Improve content to increase click-throughs by 30% by Jun 30, 20yy	30%	18%	1%	17%	9%	If new plan works, we should meet quarter targets

The plan should be a realistic assessment of likely performance. The team should look at their goal for the period and work out ways to meet it. In the Comments, the second Key Result looks like it is less likely to happen, while the team at least has a plan for the last KR.

An honest appraisal of the current situation and plan is better than unrealistic optimism.

Other Components of Review Preparation

The final step involves putting together information about the market, competition, highlights of the period, and any graphs and visuals that you feel best explain your progress. When reviews are done weekly, this is typically one—two slides. When presentations are made to the board, for example, there is a lot of work that goes into preparing researched information about changes in the environment.

As a reviewer, you will be more effective if you are prepared. Usually, this means that you have gone through the data prior to the meeting and have defined your areas of focus.

During the Review

There are five elements to an effective review, usually done in sequence:

1. Overview: This gives an opportunity for the reviewer and others to understand the overall business and its environment
2. Update on actions or projects agreed in the last review: This completes the cycle of problem-solving. Once the reviewer and the reviewee agree on an action, it must be completed.
3. Presentation of performance with reasons for gaps, and solutions for closing them: This is the part of the review the most time should be spent on to ensure that the root causes are understood and the plan made to reduce gaps is the best one possible.
4. Presentation of plan for the next period: If the cadence is a week, then this should be the plan for the next week. These plans should incorporate the impact of actions taken to close gaps.
5. Summary: A statement of the major decisions and actions agreed during the review. Actions should have a description, person responsible and expected completion date. Occasionally, there may be a connected set of activities that need to be completed over a longer period. These should be highlighted as Projects.

As a reviewer, you will need to prioritize what needs to be focussed on. Addressing one–two areas in detail during each review is the best way to continually improve performance and provide support as needed.

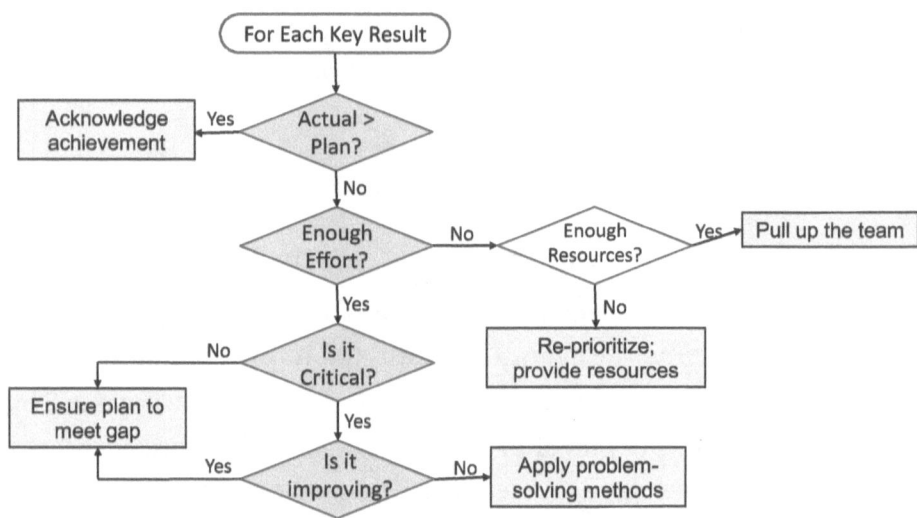

The flowchart given here provides a structure on what to address and how. There are four key questions that need to be asked:

1. Is the performance better than what was planned? If so, acknowledge the achievement and move to the next Key Result.
2. Has there been enough effort put in to meet the plan? If not, check if the team had enough resources. If they did not, either provide the necessary resources or reprioritize the task so they can either devote more time to this activity or not do it at all during the period. If they did have enough resources but still did not do it, it is important to communicate that this is not acceptable.
3. Is the Key Result critical? While it is a 'Key Result', which means that it is an important measure, there will always be some measures more important than others. If this is not an important one, even if the gap is large, verify the plan.
4. Is it improving? Even if it is a critical Key Result, if it is improving over the previous period, it is an indication that the solutions are working. Again, verify the plan and move on. If, however, it is not improving, it needs more attention. Ideally, the reviewer

will already have completed a problem-solving exercise. In these cases, verify that the right cause(s) have been identified. Set up another meeting if required to ensure that this activity is done properly.

After the Review

Once the review is complete, the reviewee ensures that the agreed actions are circulated to all the people in the review and then implements all the agreed action plans.

Depending on the cadence of the review, as a reviewer, you may want to check in on the completion of important actions before the next review.

Program/Project Reviews

While business reviews are held for every entity, program reviews are done only for your strategic programs or other projects. The principles and guidelines remain the same as described earlier.

Participants in the review are the team members identified for the program, and often a supervising manager. For company-level strategic programs, the supervising manager is usually the CEO.

The purpose of this review is to monitor the progress of the specific program. Strategic programs usually involve many tasks and activities, and they often engage people from different departments. Additionally, the impact of the program (scope of effect) is usually far beyond the scope of the teams participating in the program (scope of control). Hence there is often the chance of conflict during the development and deployment of each program.

For example, a new program for increasing sales productivity may be developed by a small team in the company headquarters, but it will impact each salesperson working across the company. Business units may have reservations about the impact of changes on salespeople retention. Senior management intervention may be required for effective implementation of measures. Strategic programs often need support and guidance of senior leadership to succeed.

The document used to review a program is like the one used in defining the program. We had discussed the format earlier. The third section of the format was as given:

No	Significant Activities	Who	When
4	Meet 25 customers for feedback on the new plan	Priya	Oct 25
5	Obtain approval from finance for new incentive scheme	Arun	Oct 30

During the review, this section has two additional columns:

No	Significant Activities	Who	When	% Complete	Status
4	Meet 25 customers for feedback on the new plan	Priya	Oct 25	60%	Met 15 customers (Green)
5	Obtain approval from finance for new incentive scheme	Arun	Oct 30	10%	(Red)

While Priya's task is going well and is expected to be finished on time, Arun has been able to meet with the finance folks only once, and they have cancelled subsequent meetings. In such a case, you may want to get senior management support to get either an approval or clarity on why the approval is not forthcoming.

Programs are usually focussed on meeting objectives in the medium or longer term, while business reviews are usually focussed on results in that quarter. While issues with business reviews are usually urgent, program issues are frequently more important. It is, hence, vital to prioritize both.

Reporting Systems

If you follow management systems like OKR or BSC, there are a range of software solutions available for setting objectives and measures, for communication and for decision-making.

If your company has a small number of people, using Microsoft Excel or Google Sheets can work well. When it must be deployed across a large organization, however, subscribing to a paid application or building it as an add on to your existing system is usually advisable.

For your Management Process to be successful, you will need access to good data. We have already discussed the importance of collecting data at the right amount of detail and collecting data only to the level required for proper decision-making.

In most early stages of organizations, internal systems are a mish mash of a few paid systems like accounting and inventory management, along with CRM software, while the rest are homegrown applications and spreadsheets. Together these are called the Management Information System or MIS of the company. In large organizations, this is important enough to have a Chief Information Officer (CIO) responsible for the design and maintenance of internal company information.

Usual signs that the reporting systems are not optimal are as follows:

1. A plethora of dashboards, with individuals needing to look at or contribute to upwards of three dashboards to get their job done. Usually any new program or project has its own tracking dashboard, often with overlapping information available in others.
2. Many reports, with anyone being able to create a publicly available report. People create their own reports—many for a one-time use—and that adds to the available reports. There is also usually no index or information about which report should be used for what purpose.
3. Lack of a standardized format for regular reviews. During a review, people use their own templates, sources and data elements.

Until you can relook at the entire reporting system, here are some things you can do:

1. The dashboards are usually customizable. Remove the ones you do not need. If they are not customizable, start with the decision you are seeking to make and identify the elements that will help you. Do not spend any time on the rest of the elements.

2. For your team, create an internal page (can be an email), listing the reports they should look at, and provide links where possible so they do not need to navigate the system to see them.
3. For reviews, you could use the templates recommended in this chapter.

It is a common misconception that being able to work with data is an innate ability and that some people have it and others do not. While it is true that some people relate to numbers better than others, it is also true that everyone can be trained to understand how to use a good set of reports.

> *Anyone can be trained to use a good set of reports effectively.*

How to Make Effective Reports

Operational reports for a system are more effective if they are developed after answering four questions:

1. What decisions or actions need to be taken based on this system?
2. What could be the reasons leading to that decision or action?
3. What information can help in taking that decision or action?
4. What comparisons or summaries are needed?

Let's take an example for a system designed for inside sales, where agents call into prospects to sell a product. The purpose of the system is to increase sales and sales productivity.

Examples of decisions or actions can be as follows:

- Training: Which sales agents need to be trained, and on what should they be trained?
- Time-on-task: What can an agent do to improve their effective call time?

- Bottom Few: Who are the consistent non-performers who need to be let go?
- Lead Quality: Do I need to improve the quality of leads?

Let's consider the first decision. Here are two possible reasons for training, along with the information that can help:

- An agent is not using the system correctly or efficiently, and hence is taking longer to make calls. The information required here is the time between calls.
- Agent is not able to move fast enough from one stage to another. The information required here could be the days spent at each stage of the funnel, and the average number and duration of calls made at each stage of the funnel.

And finally, consider the summaries or comparisons required to select agents for training and identify what training they need.

- Comparisons between agents will help identify those whose performance is lowest.
- A summary across productivity ranges will help identify how many people need training.

Once you have the necessary elements of information, you can organize them the way you need it. You can also decide if a visual plot of some of the data helps take decisions and can introduce graphs as needed.

Remember to always have one report that can be exported into a spreadsheet, which contains transaction-level data. In the aforementioned case, this would have the data for each call made, possibly with a link to the recording of the call. You can then use pivot tables for additional analysis.

Aligning the Organization: Epilogue

The group met again after three months to discuss Livewell's progress.

"So how is it going?" asked Kamini.

"It's been a crazy few months," said Subodh, "but we are pleased with the results. We are doing well on our Breakthrough Objectives. Our new wearable Livewell Flex is out in the market with limited coverage, and the doctors are loving it. Our pre-orders have already exceeded 2,000 units."

"Yes, I have been seeing that in your monthly report," said Kriti. "It's amazing that you are progressing well on all fronts. That's rare to see."

"Thanks," said Ankit. "Some of this was certainly because of the alignment of the entire team. The OKR rollout was surprisingly easy after the first month. Javed helped us a lot in ironing out the kinks. We were somewhat apprehensive about making all the objectives transparent. For example, we wondered how salespeople would react to seeing a company-level Breakthrough Objective of reducing the salesperson turnover.

They took it very well, though. There were a lot of jokes, especially when HR mapped their objectives with this. But in the last quarter, our salesperson turnover reduced by half. We may still not meet the number for the year, but we may be at a lower run rate."

"How did the Balanced Scorecard turn out?" interrupted Kriti.

"It was an interesting exercise. We first spent several hours on it. By the time we were done, we had run out of wall space. Then we figured there were too many measures and called in the rest of the management team to help us cull it down to the measures that we all agreed were important. They really engaged with it, especially the parts where they saw their own contribution. They pointed out links that we had not seen. We finally ended up with 26 measures," said Subodh.

"Interesting," said Kriti. "Now coming to OKRs. Can you share some of them with us? It would be nice to see what you came up with."

"Yes, that was the plan anyway," said Ankit. "You remember the Breakthrough Objectives we came up with? Well we used those as company-level objectives for the quarter and came up with the Key Results for them. Here they are."

Ankit projected the Objectives and Key Results.

Objective 1. Expand the doctor network.

- Key Result 1: Enhance the doctor app to reflect all key parameters by August 15
- Key Result 2: Create a doctor kit by August 1
- Key Result 3: Sign up 400 doctors, each with at least 50 patients by September 30

Objective 2. Increase sales of Livewell Flex.

- Key Result 1: Release Livewell Flex for production by August 31
- Key Result 2: Launch Livewell Flex in two cities by September 30
- Key Result 3: Obtain pre-orders for 1,000 Livewell Flex devices by September 30

Objective 3. Reduce turnover of sales team.

- Key Result 1: Launch a new sales incentive program by July 31
- Key Result 2: Assign a coach to every salesperson missing their June 30 sales targets by July 15
- Key Result 3: Ensure that less than five salespersons resign between July 1 and September 30

They all spent a few minutes reviewing the OKRs. "Nice", said Kriti. "I notice that these key results are the same as the programs we had in the strategy matrix. I also notice that the target dates of the key results are within the coming quarter. Is that intentional?"

"Yes", said Subodh. "Our OKRs are for the quarter, and so are the measures. We decided to stay with only the Breakthrough Objectives at the company level. That may not be continued in future. We adjusted the target values to reflect this quarter. Hence, we took on the goal for

400 doctor sign-ups, pre-orders for Livewell Flex and a headcount of the salespeople."

"I see. So, you have called out the specific important focus area for this quarter and put it as a key result. You may or may not have it again for the next quarter," asked Kamini.

"Precisely," said Subodh. "You have got it. We also published our personal OKRs. It's important for the company to understand that we all have specific tasks as well. Let me share one with you. I decided to directly support adding new doctors. I took that as one of my objectives."

Subodh Objective. Doctor engagement program.

- Key Result 1: Meet with 20 doctors and get feedback on the proposed program and Livewell Flex by July 20
- Key Result 2: Accompany salespeople for at least 50 doctor visits by Sept 25
- Key Result 3: Conduct a webinar for doctors by Sept 30.

"Wow, that looks ambitious," said Kriti. "Should you not be taking goals that will send a message that goals must be met."

"We are taking the opposite direction, actually," said Subodh. "We want people to have stretch goals and to try and meet them. It's OK to reach say 70% of your goals if they are ambitious enough. In fact, if someone meets all their OKRs, we review them to see if they are a bit too easy."

"This is just the tip of the iceberg," said Ankit. "We put this out for everyone to view and asked if people wanted to participate in any of these projects. We had more than 50 volunteers by the end of the day. Putting together cross-functional teams was a breeze. The program owners for our strategic programs could not be happier. As an example, one of our top salespersons came to me to request a coach—she wanted to improve further. Now everyone wants one.

Then we sat down with each of our direct reports and published their OKRs. The weekly reviews with them is now a breeze. We know what to talk about and how to move forward. It really has made our lives both easier and more focused."

Kriti said, "One thing that concerns me is that focusing on this quarter only can mean that we lose the big picture. Don't get me wrong, I love quarterly results. But I also don't want that to be the sole driving force. Is it possible to run a marathon as a series of sprints?"

"That is an extremely insightful question," said Javed. "I must remember your question and the way you have phrased it for future sessions. While the image it conjures is effective, it is not what is happening here. If I were to modify your analogy somewhat, our Mission, Vision and Core Strategy define how we will run our race. But this is a race where the track is not predefined. You cannot plan to complete it. At every turn, the contours of the track can change. If there is a water body, you may need to swim through it. If your plan is annual, you will try and run through it. Our quarterly plans recognize that the course changes are faster than before, so we need to change our plans sooner than earlier."

Kriti nodded, "Great response, thanks Javed."

Ankit continued, "Thanks, Javed. That was useful, and a perfect segue to the review process. We set up a weekly review process. People went crazy when we first informed them. We tried explaining that this should save them time, but it did not help. Finally, Subodh and I had to request them to just try if for four weeks. If it did not work, we would change the reviews to monthly.

The first two weeks were crazy. But it's taken surprisingly little time to settle down, and we are already more or less used to this cadence. There are still occasional hiccups. But people like that we are getting together to help solve their problems on a regular basis. And we are finding that our time is being better used."

"Seems like it's really working for you then," said Kamini.

Javed smiled. His only contribution had been to respond to Kriti's question. Ankit and Subodh had taken over the meeting completely.

SECTION 4
Building your Culture

Culture eats Strategy for Breakfast

– Peter Drucker

Prologue: Building Your Culture

It has been a year since Ankit and Subodh first met Javed, and they were both reflecting on how far they had come. Their fledgling company now seemed to be well on its journey to success. The Vision they had set for themselves was still far away, but these days everything seemed doable. They had met 85% of their OKRs the last quarter.

Kamini started off the meeting by saying, "Livewell seems to be meeting or ahead of most of your commitments. In our internal meeting, you are among the stars of our portfolio. We would like to invite you to speak at our next summit. I think we can all learn from your experience."

"Thanks. Both Subodh and I would be delighted to come," Ankit said.

Kamini had been looking at Subodh. "You don't seem to be your usual chipper self. Is something worrying you?"

"It's not a worry exactly, but for the past few weeks I have been feeling that the system is running away from us a bit. Raghav, one of our salesmen, pitched a solution that we don't provide at present. I counselled him and he agreed not to do it, but he did not seem to think that it was a problem. And folks from our customer service teams have been promising a special prize for the winner of lucky draw to customers. There is no lucky draw, but they figure that no one will know, and it helps them get better customer ratings. I have been wondering for a while if we are growing too fast," Said Subodh.

Javed said. "I'm glad you brought this up. I have also found that while the entire team is committed to meeting their numbers, there is a somewhat casual approach towards commitments. This will likely result in us losing our customers' trust and our reputation. As a company grows, its culture starts to shift. It starts as a reflection of the founders' values, but for the culture to be sustained, it needs to be accepted and owned by the team."

Kamini was looking thoughtful. "You know, as doctors we take the Hippocratic Oath. Contrary to popular belief, it does not actually say 'to do no harm', but it's a set of covenants that we all agree to live with. It is in effect a set of values that we must all try and live by. It should all be obvious, but by taking the oath we commit to its guidelines."

"I couldn't have put it better myself," said Javed.

"So, what's next? How do we put together something that clearly explains the values that we should all abide by? Javed, this was your fourth lever, wasn't it?" Now that Subodh was committed, he wanted to get right to it.

Javed put up the 4 levers again.

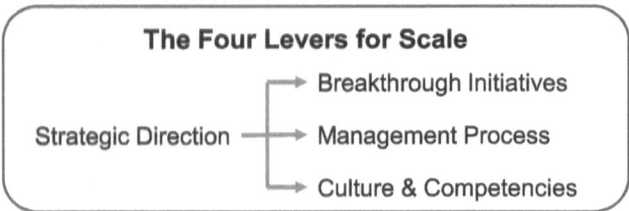

"Yes, it is the fourth lever. But notice that the lever is named Culture and Competencies. You need to develop both. Your people need to be eager to build Livewell and also have the capabilities needed to do it—as the idiom goes, employees should be both 'willing and able'."

Kamini added, "And it is the right thing to do as well. We want to build an organization everyone is proud of, including our employees. As Livewell grows, our employees should grow along with us."

Everyone nodded.

Javed then put up the expanded diagram.

Lever 4. Culture and Competencies

"To start with, we need to know what kind of culture you want. And that starts from your Core Values. We need to uncover what they are. Like our Mission, our Core Values must come from the heart. It is important that these are not merely words. As we formulate them, we will need to look for stories from within us that support our values.

Once we have uncovered our values, we need to make sure our policies support our values. For example, if we say our customers come first, then we should have clear policies, with budgets to back them, that allow our employees to go out of their way to help a customer."

"I like this idea," said Subodh. "I have been to companies with written down Core Values, but the people I spoke to did not know much about them. I like that we will use stories to explain them, and back them with policies so everyone knows we are serious."

"I can see how this will help address the ethical issues that I mentioned earlier. But it seems a bit simplistic to say we have established a culture if all we have is a set of values and nothing to back them up," said Ankit.

"Let's not underestimate the power of values and policies. Our policies should include rituals—things we will do regularly to bring people together. You will be surprised what a statement of values backed up by policies and stories can do. Especially if you communicate it well and regularly, and each of you live it and ensure others do too," said Javed.

"I can back that," said Kriti. "At the heart of a culture is trust, and what Javed just mentioned supports that. Unlike everything else about which we have spoken so far, culture is a soft issue. It can develop organically or can be set back by a single wrong hire at a senior level. It's also extremely hard to define."

Kamini was looking at her phone. "Well here is a definition. Organizational culture is defined as the underlying beliefs, assumptions, values and ways of interacting that contribute to the unique social and psychological environment of an organization. And this is pretty much what Kriti just explained."

"Thanks, Kamini," said Ankit. "I can see now that this is going to take continuous effort to keep up. But it seems like it will be worth it."

"You will also need to back it up with developing your people, specially your leaders. Not just on the culture aspect but the overall development of core skills, including management skills."

"Yeah, Ruchika, our HR head has been talking about some formal development programs for some time. It does not seem like it should be a big priority at this time. We have great people, and they are doing a good job," said Subodh.

"Yes, they are," said Ankit. "We now have about a thousand people working for the company. I don't think we need a full-fledged learning function in the company just yet, but it would be worth while exploring options to keep our people current. Let's get started with working on our values. We will get to people development following that."

"I suggest you speak to your teams, especially those who have been with you from the start. Discuss values with them and ask them for examples within the company when these were upheld and where they were not. Start with the Mission Statement and go from there. Once you have a bunch of stories and ideas, lets meet up and craft our Core Values."

"Sounds like a plan," said Ankit.

Building a Work Culture: Values and Policies

When a company is initially set up, its culture is defined by its founders. They may not formally articulate their values, but they live it, and their team experiences it. You will find that at the start, there will be a strong ethos within the organization. If the founders value ideas, the company will be full of people contributing theirs. If the founders value compliance, that will show up in the people too.

New hires to the company may not share the same values as the founders. As the company grows, the original set of values start to dissipate. New managers come in with their own set of values. Some come from companies with a vastly different culture that starts to rub off on their team, attracting others who share these values. As the culture evolves organically, it can take many shapes and forms. Different parts of the company start to behave differently.

A cohesive company culture impacts performance in many ways. The most obvious is employee satisfaction and hence performance. If your organization has a strong culture, employees feel valued and happy if they are aligned with the culture. They tend to be loyal and to support the organization's goals. The impact goes far beyond the employees as well. Customers experience better service and vendors feel more valued.

In one company known for its informal and effective culture, a new manager came from a system where he was used to more discipline. His team bonded well together and delivered on their goals, but the team members would come in and leave at different times. Hence meetings would only be held after lunch when all employees were present. The new manager believed that coming to office on time was vital. When repeated requests did not get compliance, he instituted a policy to sign in and out, with late coming resulting in half-day absenteeism.

When that failed to ensure compliance as well, he withheld their salaries till they signed in. This effectively destroyed the existing culture and a few top performers left. The manager was soon moved out of the division, but the damage had been done. Many workplaces follow strict adherence to office timings, and others do not. There is no right or wrong implied. But if the culture is established, changing it suddenly will impact everyone.

As you can see from the example, there can be two views and both can be right, but for different companies. One view is adopted by most tech companies today in that the time an employee comes in or leaves is not as important as their independence and quality of work. The other is vitally important in say a BPO company, where discipline is critical and being late can affect customer requirements.

Case Study of a Strong Culture: The HP Way

When Bill Hewlett and Dave Packard set up HP, they realized the importance of having a common set of values. In the 1990s, HP was 'the' technology company to emulate in Silicon Valley. They were easily the most innovative and forward-thinking organization of the day. Their values are encoded in 'The HP Way'. There are five statements, each with an explanation.

1. We have trust and respect for Individuals
2. We focus on a high level of achievement and contribution
3. We conduct our business with uncompromising integrity
4. We achieve our common objectives through teamwork
5. We encourage flexibility and innovation

For HP, these were not just words, but were values they lived by. Their employee loyalty was remarkably high, and as a result they had low attrition. Other companies were happy to hire people from HP. Phrases like 'my heart beats HP blue' were used by employees and ex-employees with pride. HP provided a lot of freedom to their managers, and multiple entities were set up, each with their ability to be innovative in their area of choice. Individuals were passionate about the work they did and HP quality was a byword in the industry.

HP had many innovations to look after their people. They were pioneers in establishing a health insurance plan for all employees in 1942, giving employees stock in the company if they had served more than six months in 1957, and introducing flexitime in 1973. While the values were set, units interpreted them in their own way, with new examples and stories of innovative application of the principles. Till the late 1980s, HP was a star with few parallels.

But as HP grew, they made some errors in strategy. They continued to focus on hardware when customers were asking for solutions. HP started to slow down and competitors specifically Dell started to make major inroads. In the late 1990s, the board brought in Carly Fiorina as the CEO. She discarded the HP Way, and brought in many changes including merging many of the units and firing a lot of people. She also acquired Compaq, which turned out to be far less successful than hoped. In effect, the HP Way was not compatible with Carly's approach.

Since then, HP has been through several CEOs, and has been split into two separate companies HP Inc and HP Enterprises. They are still large but are no longer the force they used to be. More recently, they seem to be again recommitting to the HP Way and are once again beating market expectations. While growth is slow, the company may once again become a major force.

There are several lessons to be learned from HP, about consequences of a strong culture:

1. Building a strong culture requires a set of values. These values cannot just be written on a piece of paper; they must be actively pursued.
2. A strong culture can create a highly effective organization, with high loyalty, and high employee retention.

3. The culture can be highly innovative and customer focussed. It can provide customers with the assurance of continued great service.
4. Trying to go against a strong existing culture is like swimming against a strong undercurrent.
5. A strong culture cannot counter poor strategy. While hindsight is always 20:20, IBM was able to reinvent itself as a solutions company and continues to be a major player in the industry, while HP stayed a predominantly hardware provider.

Living Your Values

A consulting firm has a value of "We will follow the highest levels of integrity in everything that we do." They are serious about all their values and live by them. At one point they had a problem with their phone connection. This was before cell phones were ubiquitous, so the company landline was an important resource. The linesman who was assigned to fix it, came, and asked for a small bribe.

The company refused, escalated the issue, and pursued it with the superiors in the telecom department. However, after a month there was still no action. The company then paid the bribe, and the phone was restored.

In their next meeting, the CEO proposed that they modify the value under question to read as: "We will follow the highest levels of integrity in everything that we do with our customers, suppliers and between ourselves," so that when there was a situation like that of the linesman, it would not violate the value. However, the chairman did not allow it. The point he made was that there will be times when you will violate a value. But the important thing is to reflect on it, not take the easy way out, and not normalize it.

Living your values may have financial implications. For example, at NIIT, one of their Core Values was: "We will meet any and every commitment made to society, irrespective of any cost that may have to be incurred." One of the ways this was implemented was that in any customer project, commitment by any individual would be honoured.

In one instance, a manager made a costing error in a project and proposed to a customer that it would be delivered at around 40% of the correct price. When the mistake was realized, it was brought to the customer's notice, who insisted that NIIT must deliver as proposed. Instead of walking away from the project, NIIT completed it. This and other stories were provided as examples for each of NIITs values.

Setting Up Organization Values

When writing down your values, you need to consider both the existing culture of your company and what you would like your company to stand for. You should do it in three steps.

Step 1. Collect Stories

The existing culture in any company is best understood by listening to the stories shared by those employees who have been in the company for a long time.

> *Your existing culture is best understood by listening to stories shared by long-term employees.*

To find the existing company culture, you need to listen to the war stories of people, find out what they like about the company and what they think about management. This is best done in a relatively informal setting with homogenous groups of people who know each other, and asking them for incidents and events that to them reflect the values of the company. It is important to do this at all levels of the organization hierarchy. Do not record the meetings; when people are being recorded, they tend to share less. You could jot down a sentence or two periodically to remember a story.

Once the stories are completed, you can ask them what is unique about the company and what they like about working here. This can be recorded, and you can take detailed notes and ask for examples. Document the stories you have collected with nuances and names immediately after the meeting. Take photographs of the participants. Prepare a deck with the photographs and audio (if recorded), along with quotes of why people like working in the company.

Step 2. Senior Management Workshop

Bring the top management of the team together. Run the deck you have prepared, narrating the stories you have heard. Take the time to tell the stories well. Then share the quotes of why people like working at your company. You second last slide of the deck should be the Mission Statement. The last slide should have one question: "What is important about our company and what is unique about working here?"

Participants should then write down their answers on post-it notes. Group the notes into similar ideas and label each group. You are likely to end up with seven—eight groups if you start with about 25 ideas. Encourage discussion around each of the ideas. Ideally you should narrow the ideas down to five or six. Once you have them, revisit the deck to make sure that the voice of employees has been considered. The list is now your Core Values.

The values now need to be described, so that the meaning is unambiguous. Use the list of ideas to add colour to the statement of values. Link a story or two to each of the values, so that they connect with employees.

Step 3. Socialize the Values

Meet a few groups of employees and take them through the Core Values along with the descriptions and examples. Ask for their opinion and whether they have additional stories to support the values.

Finally, collate the major employee issues and discuss it with the CEO and the senior management team. There may be minor changes, but if the process has been done well, you will usually find that employees will resonate with the values. You will usually end up making the descriptions better, and some of the statements may be changed to resonate better. Once this exercise is completed, you will have your Core Values.

Policies Supporting Your Core Values

Once your Core Values are written down, you will find that there are some values that require your company to have specific policies to support them. For example, if your company has a Core Value around innovation, what will the company do to foster it? Will there be recognition for innovation? Will there be a budget? Will the company provide its employees with time to work on innovation projects?

Answering these questions are critical to Core Values. If there is no support from the organization in actual policies and schemes, values end up being just words. Policies show how committed management is to the values that they have created.

Taking another example from NIIT, another value of theirs was: "We will foster career-building by creating opportunities that demand learning, thinking and innovation from each one of us." This was supported by a whole host of HR initiatives including aggressive training mandates for each team. Training days were consciously measured and socialized, and people were frequently moved across divisions to give them more opportunity to grow.

Communicating Your Core Values

The approach to communication of Core Values should be to provide an opportunity for every employee to relate to them. It can be done one-on-one (usually a good idea when hiring a senior person into the company) or can be part of an induction program. At NIIT, during induction of new employees, the session on communicating values was the only one that would only be conducted by a business head or a C level executive.

When communicating values, start by explaining how they were uncovered. Then explain each value using examples both from your personal experience in the company and some of the stories that were used to come up with the value. Following that, explain the policies the company has to support the value. Finally, ask the audience to come up with examples that they can personally relate to. For new employees, these may be from their earlier companies or from their personal life.

It is important to recognize that adhering to values is always a work-in-progress. There will always be some conflict between how each person relates to your Core Values and their original intent. At the start, employees may ask questions that may not have obvious answers are not obvious. It is vital to acknowledge these questions, encourage a discussion and be open to acknowledge where there is no clear answer.

It is also possible that employees will cite cases where a Core Value was not followed, perhaps even by senior managers. For values to survive, each case must be addressed and the result should be communicated appropriately. The continuous discussion around your values are what make them alive. Acknowledging a slip in values is giving the message that values are important.

Once employees have been taken through a discussion on values. It is a good idea to make it available and visible in several ways. It can be part of your internal website or included in your newsletter. Depending on your organization, you may also choose to put up the Statement of Values on walls within the company.

Your HR department should be chartered with continual reinforcement of values. This should ideally not be a direct and repeated communication of the values but rather should be done in activities and stories that reinforce the values. These stories should be a necessary part of employee communication.

Building Organization Competence

For your company to be successful, bringing in, growing, and retaining talent is critical. The quality of its employees will define the company's ambition, and its ability to grow and thrive in a competitive environment.

Through the 1990s and early 2000s, Airtel built a management team that was the envy of their competitors. They attracted the best talent available within the industry and brought in others from the FMCG industry. Attracting the best people was important enough to reflect in their Vision Statement. Their Vision in 2005 was to become a top brand in the country, which included 'attract the best talent', as a part of it. Where skills were not readily available (in the early days it was in the technology), they brought in people from Europe and the United States.

But bringing in good talent is only part of the story—your company must build skills from within as well. The largest and most diversified group in India, the Tata Group, hires from the top business schools. They hire both for their individual companies as well as for the Tata Administrative Services (TAS). They select high performing youngsters across their companies for this program. Students joining TAS, are rotated across various companies for a year and then fast-tracked to a management position in one of those companies. This program is highly sought after since the experience is great and each person in the TAS is mentored by a senior executive at one of the Tata Group companies.

Football clubs understand this process very well. On one hand, they hire the best players they can attract, and on the other, they have a youth selection program to bring in talent early. Lionel Messi, arguably one of the greatest footballers of this generation, joined Barcelona through their youth program.

In earlier chapters, we have covered some of the essentials in attracting and retaining the best people for one's company. A shared Vision is one such essential. A great organization culture is another. Demonstrating commitment to the growth of people is a third.

Skill Development and Knowledge Enhancement

Most people are naturally inclined towards learning new things from a wide variety of sources. In personal life, this could be learning a new recipe or pursuing a new hobby. Within the organization, learning is continuously required as new products, competitors and business models emerge. A learning organization is better able to respond to changes in the market and in its customers.

The growth of social media has changed the way we consume information. Content is created at rates that were earlier only imagined in science fiction, and consumption of information is becoming ever more bite-sized and image-based. Traditional learning functions of organizations have mostly been slow to adapt to this.

As a start-up in the process of becoming a large organization, or a division within a bigger organization wanting to build a learning function, there are a few principles that will help in building a learning organization.

Embrace the OSF Ratio

The proportion of time spent by an employee between **O**n-the-job learning, **S**ocial learning, and **F**ormal learning is called the OSF ratio. This is not a validated mathematical model, but instead is a guideline based on interviews of successful executives. While this varies from company to company, and from role to role, it is often called the 70:20:10 rule.

70% of learning comes from experience on the job, 20% from social (including from colleagues) learning and 10% from formal training.

> *The OSF ratio is a rule of thumb that states that 70% of learning comes from on-the-job experience, 20% from social learning and 10% from formal training.*

Once you recognize this, you can create an environment where you support all kinds of learning, and not just the formal kind. The next few sections cover how to do that.

You Do Need a Learning Management System (LMS), But Keep It Open

Learning Management Systems (LMSs) along with Learning Content Management Systems (LCMSs) have four important functions that are needed for an effective learning organization:

1. The ability to store and serve content.
2. The ability to assess knowledge and keep score.
3. The ability to allow learners to interact with one another.
4. The ability to track the learning of individuals and provide relevant reports.

Historically, tracking employee learning was the most prized function of an LMS, because it offered management (and more specifically the learning function) more control over what everyone was learning and the ability to link this learning to performance appraisal and individual growth. Content was developed using specific standards so everything could be tracked properly.

While tracking of learning continues to remain important, traditional LMSs are difficult to set up and need tight integration with HR systems. It is difficult to both create and modify content as well. Today, look for a more open system. Important features of this system should be as follows:

1. There should be a strong search function that allows employees to query the content database and find learning nuggets that they need. Employees can choose what they want to learn.
2. Anyone should be able to form a group for training and to invite others in the organization to participate.
3. It should be easy to create a training program using a mix of content including documents and videos.

Separate Learning Content from Assessment of Learning; Keep It Modular

When computer-based training first became a reality, a guiding principle in content creation was the level of interactivity within each course. During course development, a rule of thumb was to have one interaction every four frames, which frequently was a question. That was a useful rule when content was relatively static, and a program once developed would run for several years.

Today, given the need to continually update content, the approach should be different.

- Content should be as modular as possible. Ideally, have a single idea or concept in one module lasting between 3 and 15 minutes. For a course, string together several modules, but make them individually accessible later as well.
- Keep the content separate from the assessment. For example, an engineer may want to study the specifications of a product in detail and is happy to read a lengthy document, but a salesperson wants to know just enough to be able to sell it and may learn more from videos showing interactions with customers. It does not matter how someone learns something, as long as they do learn.

Once you separate the assessment system, you have the option of leaving the learning completely open for employees. For example, you could have a quiz on costs of alternate transport systems and let employees run a Google search to prepare.

Let Everyone Create Content; Create Incentives

Video content is the easiest to consume, and it is quite easy to create. Additionally, people enjoy creating these videos. Teams can create content on a wide range of areas, from induction programs for new recruits to new product training or even using new systems. Some of these can be created by the departments formally.

Allow authorship of content. This makes sure that people feel proud when their content is seen by others. Also allow viewers of content to rate it. Your search engine can give a higher priority while showing content that has a higher rating and viewership. Over time, this self-selection will ensure that poor content does not come up for viewing.

You can add further incentives by assigning points for successful videos and providing recognition or even reward to content that is most viewed or commented on. When you need a more structured program, you can select some of these videos in addition to content prepared specifically for the course.

For Professionally Created Content, Focus on Critical Mistakes

In the mid-1990s, a team of professors at the Northwestern University, came up with an idea for adult learning. Conventional wisdom is that training should be developed to meet learning objectives. This team posited that training should be developed to reduce errors. They developed a model called Critical Mistakes Analysis to determine mistakes made in different environments.

You can apply this concept very effectively for updating your employees' skills. For example, your review of your salesperson shows he becomes very defensive if your customer raises a strong objection. If this 'critical mistake' can have specific training for correcting it, it would be useful not just for that specific salesperson but for several other salespeople as well.

Content for this training is usually scenario-based. A scenario is created where the mistake is shown. The learner is encouraged to select a specific action. They are given feedback on that action and are required to reflect on why their selection was right or wrong. Thereafter a discussion or presentation can detail the mistake and summarize the learning.

Assess the Application of Concepts or Facts Rather than the Concepts or Facts Themselves

Multiple choice questions are a good format to use to check if learning has happened. They can be easily created without professional assistance. When assessing, it is better to check for application rather than recall alone.

For example, here are two ways to test a for concept knowledge:

Option 1. What is the best setting for low-light photography?
   a. Wide aperture with fast shutter speed
   b. Narrow aperture with fast shutter speed
   c. Wide aperture with slow shutter speed
   d. Narrow aperture with slow shutter speed

Option 2. You have been taking photographs at a heritage site, but the sun is setting, and it is getting dark. You want to take a few more pictures. What will you do for best results?
   a. Increase your camera aperture while retaining your fast shutter speed
   b. Decrease your camera aperture while retaining your fast shutter speed
   c. Increase your camera aperture and reduce your shutter speed
   d. Decrease your camera aperture and reduce your shutter speed

The second question in this case is simply reframed as an application question to demonstrate the difference. Also, notice that there are multiple correct answers here. The learner must select the 'best' option, requiring them to compare and apply.

Integrate Elements of Social Media; Preferably Integrate Existing Tools

People can learn from one another very effectively. Some ways of effectively providing for social learning include the following:

1. A social network with all employees where people can ask questions and get answers. This can be something as simple as WhatsApp groups or Work Chats, or other popular tools.
2. Blogs and podcasts by employees where the company can promote certain content and encourage participation.
3. Expert stand-up sessions or webinars.
4. Documents prepared by employees that can support training in your searchable learning database.

Social media methods can also help make on-the-job learning more effective. If employees can easily post questions on an online board and receive immediate answers, you have an effective learning organization.

Everyone Loves a Certificate

In cases where you need to impart formal skills to employees, you do not need to develop your own training programs. Organizations like EDX, Udemy and others have associations with top universities to provide courses and certificates. You can decide the skills you want to promote among your employees and can come up with a scheme where you partially or fully support the fees of these programs for employees.

The advantage here is that you do not have to incur the cost of developing the training, and it will always be current. Most of these courses will have academic rigour and be run by a top faculty from a well-known university. For example, a micro-masters certificate from Columbia University on Data Analytics can be something that your employees will aspire to complete. To make sure these are not misused, agree to pay a percentage of the costs (perhaps 80%), but on the condition that the student passes the exam.

You can create your own internal certificates as well. Though not as universally recognized, employees will still value these as evidence of having completed a formal program.

Employee Morale and Belongingness

Thus far we have addressed issues of alignment. We started with the company Mission and Vision, looked at Core Strategies, and aligned Objectives and Programs, and methods of deployment. We then addressed how values supported by policies can provide a sense of belonging and loyalty, and can further support coherence.

The power of belonging is hard to ignore. I remember a case where a person had a bad accident but refused to go to the operating theatre until he met his operating manager. Doctors thought it was because he was worried about the expenses of the treatment and tried to reassure him that his company accident policy would cover it. But that was not what he was worried about. When his operating manager came, he wanted to be sure to give him his computer password and explain where he had saved the file that would be required in a customer presentation the next day.

Your employees spend nearly half their waking hours working for your company. After their family life, it is their most significant relationship. If they feel they belong and want to contribute towards the company's success, it helps both your company and your employees. In this chapter, we will touch upon the other aspects of belongingness.

Diversity and Inclusiveness

A 2020 McKinsey study titled "Diversity wins: How inclusion matters" highlights that companies with high diversity and inclusiveness perform significantly better than those that do not have it. Companies in the top quartile of diversity (both gender and ethnic) tended to outperform those in the bottom quartile by 25% or more.

It is now evident that diversity promotes creativity, alternate perspectives and better decision-making skills. People with different backgrounds and experiences provide a wider range of alternatives and lead to more informed decisions.

While the results are evident, diversity is still not significant and globally is moving slower than the benefits would suggest It takes conscious sustained effort to have diversity in the company, but the results are worth it.

Promoting inclusiveness is even more difficult. It is possible to have a diversity policy to ensure your organization has a mix of gender, ethnic, physical abilities, and other elements of diversity. It is more difficult to ensure that your company is able to value and leverage this diversity. Inclusiveness means accepting different working styles, being receptive to alternate perspectives and being fair to all groups.

Building a diverse and inclusive company will require you to have policies on hiring that support this, providing sensitivity training executives and managers on dealing with diversity, and putting HR policies in place to promote and support inclusiveness.

Safety

Your employees should feel safe both physically and emotionally. If safety is missing from the company, you may not be able to elicit any real engagement for the goals of the company.

- Physical Health and Safety: A large percentage of the workforce is engaged in physical activity or work in places with hazardous equipment or materials. The standards for these are continually getting better, and complying with these standards in your organization will address these issues. Most companies having a late shift provide employee with transport after regular hours, particularly for their women employees.
- Psychological Safety: Psychological safety is a precondition for effective workplace relationships. Your employees must know that they will not be punished or humiliated for asking questions, voicing concerns and ideas or making mistakes.

You can create an environment where such participation is encouraged through management training in which the primary rule is to treat people as they themselves would like to be treated.

The other element for safely in a company is the absence of harassment. The Supreme Court of India has mandated that every company must have a sexual harassment policy and a committee that will address complaints as well as institute preventive measures. The committees are also required to have an external member. Besides implementing this, you may want to ensure regular training of employees to ensure that everyone realizes what constitutes acceptable behaviour.

Communication and Communication Systems

Workplace communication has been shown to impact productivity and employee morale. Offices should be designed to provide both formal and informal spaces where employees can physically communicate with each other. Open offices help in free and cross-functional communication, as compared to cubicles that were in style a few decades ago.

Technology and Communication

Technology has significantly impacted the ability to communicate and should form the backbone of your approach to communication within the company. Businesses now have access to company-wide tools that mirror the ones used in social media. Two of the more popular communication tools are Yammer and Slack. Another is Workplace by Facebook. Google also provides a wide range of tools for intra-company communication.

It is important to realize that the workplace is not limited to the work desk. All technologies today support mobile communication and you should adopt and promote mobile usage as a company. Texting and emails remain a common method of communication, but these are being supplemented and replaced by other workplace tools.

Webinars provide a way to communicate to a large audience. This could be a quarterly communication by a CXO or a new product update, or even a Q&A session after the rollout of a new policy. Tools such as Google Meeting, Skype and Zoom, all allow for basic interactions. If you want employees to answer a poll or use a whiteboard, then tools like WebEx and Adobe Connect are available. All these tools have options to record so others can review the meeting if they missed it.

Collaboration

Projects often engage people across the organization in different capacities. Your project teams can both track projects and deadlines and allow for groups to exchange and store information as the project progresses. Some of the more popular tools are Asana, Zoho Projects and Slack. Each of these have different strengths, and they all allow for collaboration. If yours is a more open, free-form collaborative environment, Slack would be a better fit, while Zoho Projects will suit more traditional project management with tasks and workflows.

You can set up teams for specific events, say an annual party, or a group within the company with young children who need to together run the company creche. You can also set up collaborative groups for divisions or departments. You can consider Slack or Workplace as good options for such collaboration and allow for regular communication using all possible media options. These groups for the most part function like a WhatsApp group, except for increased security and more company-based management systems.

Content for Top-Down Communication

Most organizations have methods to communicate regularly, including newsletters, website updates, webinars and broadcast calls, for management to be in regular touch with their employees.

It is always better to communicate more than less. But it's better still to communicate based on areas that are interesting to your employees.

> *When communicating, focus more on what employees want to hear, rather than what you want to say.*

Remember that in addition to facts, your communication needs to achieve the following:

- Trust: Keep employees updated on what the company is going through. Be transparent about both opportunities and risks. Employees need to trust that the company is not keeping secrets from them. Assessment should be realistic and pragmatic.
- Confidence: Employees need to feel confident that the company knows what it is doing and where it is headed. While the Vision does provide this confidence, a continuous subliminal message also helps.
- Inspiration (in good times): When everything is good, employees want to feel inspired. The Mission Statement is a good start. Frequent stories and examples help.
- Hope (in bad times): When times are not so good, employees need to feel that there is light at the end of the tunnel, that the present period will end.

For the most part, keep communications short. Fifteen minutes is better than 45. When you are talking about things that are necessary for employees to remember, make the session more interactive than you do otherwise. A manager I know would keep some bars of chocolate with her during open-house sessions. She would ask questions and then throw chocolates to whoever shouted out the answer first. The fact that her aim was notoriously poo only made this activity more fun.

Recognition

Everyone loves to be recognized. It can boost morale. Done right, it can support self-improvement. If you recognize someone for a behaviour, they are likely to repeat it. Having a wide range of recognition systems within your organization will ensure that employees feel valued.

Social media can play an important role in recognition. Acknowledging a person on LinkedIn or Facebook makes them feel special not just within the company but in their social circle as well. In addition, you should also post all recognition on any collaboration platforms within the company.

When instituting any form of recognition, remember that it must be sustained for it to become something that employees look forward to. You should also make sure that the recognition is fair and accurate. There are a few proven recognition programs.

> *Recognition must be sustained, so that employees can look forward to it.*

Annual events: These can be for major achievements where you recognize some employees for important achievements or milestones. Add citations for awards. Have many types of awards. For example, a 'hero' award can recognize a single large contribution, and a 'topper' award can be given for achieving the most in something.

- Ongoing recognition programs: These can range from achievements like 'Employee of the Month', to acknowledging an important event like a birthday. You may want to make these as mini-social events, where your team gets together with tea and snacks and the right people are recognized.
- Peer-to-peer recognition: Peer recognition programs are valued because these are given by people you work with every day. You may want to socialize these by having a 'recognition board' where employees can write a thank you to a colleague for

their help. More than other forms of recognition, peer-to-peer recognition improves team spirit and trust within teams.
- Personal recognition. In addition to formal recognition processes, just having a culture of thanking people for work done provides a positive culture. As a manager, you can acknowledge individuals in groups or personally whenever there is a positive contribution. This approach is referred to as 'catch people doing something right'. If you can spread this approach, you will find employees are happier and more trusting.

It is important to not confuse recognition with reward. For example, the top salespeople may get a bonus or a trip to an exotic destination. That is a reward and will hopefully motivate other salespeople to try for it next year. Anything with significant monetary value always has the possibility of causing envy and hence of becoming counter-productive to the purpose of recognition.

Rituals and Fun

Over time, organizations develop rituals that become ingrained into the culture of the company or team. These rituals support team bonding and are often useful in integrating new employees. In the technology start-up Safetipin, everything revolves around food. Employees bring something back every time they have a holiday or travel on work; all birthdays, anniversaries, weather changes, are reasons to eat. When looking for a new office, a primary criterion was to have a place large enough for everyone to eat together.

In one company, the managers personally introduce new employees to every person in the division. Some companies have regular parties to celebrate achievements, where team members can socialize outside work. Many companies celebrate major festivals with decorations, activities and even competitions. Each of these rituals serve to bring employees closer together.

Not all rituals are merely about celebration or bringing people together. In one company, meetings habitually started late. A new manager had trouble with this; in his value system, coming late meant disrespecting everyone else's time. Instead of making a scene, he instituted a small financial fine for every minute the employee was late. And it would have to be paid as soon as they walked in. This amount was pooled every month to bring in snacks for everyone. Late coming dropped dramatically. More importantly, if a person were late, they would be a bit sheepish about it, and others in the meeting would smile as they put their late fee into the box. The amount was not large, but it changed the meeting culture.

To introduce rituals in your company, you will need to answer four questions:

1. Why do you want it? Be clear about its purpose. A ten-minute huddle within a team at the start of the day is a great way for other members to know what everyone is working on that day. The purpose: helping each person articulate and achieve their goals for the day.
2. Will it work with your culture? For example, you may have an annual sports day for employees. If your company has a largely younger demographic, it may work well, but not as much if there is a wide distribution in age across the company.
3. Will you be able to sustain it? Rituals should become habit-forming. If it is too hard to do or requires a lot of set up time or money, it may not be sustainable. So, if you have a monthly celebration where each person with a birthday is celebrated, you cannot miss a few months.
4. Is it inclusive? Fun and rituals should apply equally to everyone. If you are celebrating festivals, celebrate the major ones across all religions in the team. You should also consider whether everyone can take part. In one company, the annual overnight picnic had a low participation by female employees because

alcohol was freely available, and many women were not comfortable in that environment.

You may also want to add team-building exercises to further develop bonding within a team. There are a host of activities to choose from. These can involve sessions where members share their feelings towards one another or work on a common game or problem, an offsite where the team works together on some physical activity.

Building Your Culture: Epilogue

The team got together a few days later to put together their values.

"So how do we do it?" Kamini asked. "Should we just write down what we believe and then discuss it?"

"That is certainly one way to do it. Another way is to look at the values that currently exist and use that as a starting point. I spent some time with a few of the old-timers, just talking to them about what they valued in the company. Let me start by taking you through them," said Javed.

"Radhika spoke about how she really enjoyed challenges along with the freedom to implement solutions. She mentioned the time when she came to you, Ankit, with an online marketing campaign designed to sign up fifty new doctors. Apparently, after you listened to the campaign, you mentioned that it was her call but that you needed five hundred new doctors and then left before she could object.

She mentioned that she could not sleep well that night, and then started calling up all her marketing friends looking for ideas. She asked everyone for help, including folks from production and sales. The new plan took another ten days to come together. After she met her target, you smiled and said that you thought she would be able to do it. And, of course, it was the talk of the company for a week."

Ankit smiled. "I remember that one. I knew if I stayed, I would get involved in the solution and I really believed she could do it better without my involvement."

"This is a nice story", said Kamini, "but how will it reflect as a value?" This set of a discussion, which resulted in the following statement:

We challenge ourselves to perform beyond our own expectations.

"I like this," said Kamini. "We include ourselves in this statement, so it's not like management is being preachy. Also, it does reflect the ethos that I see within the company."

Kriti had a different take. "This feels like a statement from a start-up. As we grow, I am not sure this will be right. There will be many people whose job will be to do a specific set of tasks every day. Will it work if every person challenges themselves?"

Subodh responded, "I think we are encouraging people to think a bit outside the box. I do not believe everyone will want to try something new. Some may want to improve productivity or reduce defects beyond current expectations. I would be happy if this were a value for everyone."

Kriti nodded. "I see your point."

"Now that we have written down the value, we should support it with an explanation, that also suggests that the company will support this value," said Javed. It took another 15 minutes to write down the explanation.

We believe that every one of us has potential beyond our known capabilities and can realize this potential in an environment of trust and freedom. We accept that occasionally this belief may result in mistakes. We learn from them, do not repeat them, and support our people in remedying them.

"I like it, though I may regret it," said Ankit. "We are effectively communicating that there will be no consequences to mistakes, and that the company will take the associated costs. It seems like a carte blanche to do pretty much anything."

"I think you will find that people understand that they can't do what they want, and you will find that when you give people the freedom, they will self-monitor," Javed smiled.

Over the next few hours, the team discussed other stories and then did some brainstorming of their own. Javed also guided them to look at their Mission as well as a source of values. They finally came up with six values.

- We prevent health-related problems, and we will continuously innovate and contribute in this field.
- We provide doctors and individuals with comprehensive, accurate and reliable information.

- We challenge ourselves to perform beyond our own expectations.
- We achieve our common goals through teamwork and helping each other.
- We invest in building our skills and competencies uncompromisingly.
- We build our reputation by operating with complete integrity in every interaction, within and outside the company.

"While we did come up with these together, I am a bit confused now," said Kamini. "Typically, value statements that I see seem to be more towards culture and behaviour. We only have one, the last one, that seems to be in that category."

"That's a fair point," said Javed. "Many companies I know select their values from a list of generic values. But these usually become statements of what seems to be good values, not those that the company deeply believes. Everyone knows they must have integrity. By saying that it is a value is only confirming certain core social values. I am not clear how that will drive a distinctive culture within the company."

"OK, thanks. That clarifies it," Kamini nodded.

"I like that our values focus on our Mission, our customers and our people. It's a good balance," said Kriti. The others nodded as well.

"Now that we have our values, what next? How do we create a culture that reflects these values?" asked Subodh.

"It's a good question, and I will answer that in two parts. The first part has to do with how the company will support its values," said Javed.

"I don't understand that," said Ankit. "We will live it just like we expect everyone else to."

"That's very important," said Javed, "but that is you, as a leader. What about how Livewell will support it? Let me explain. Let us take the first value we came up with—'We challenge ourselves to perform beyond our expectations'. In part, Livewell has stretch OKRs where people can stretch without worrying about a poor appraisal. But another part of that is making mistakes. How will the company deal with these?"

"You know," said Subodh. "I was thinking about this an hour ago when we were working on it. We could institute a practice of writing down and sending challenges that people accepted, as well as mistakes that they made as a result. We can then talk about them in our internal forums."

"That's a nice one," said Javed. The team then worked to complete the practices they would put in place for each value."

Subodh piped up. "And what's the second thing?"

Javed smiled. "Glad you remembered. I was coming around to it. The second is to communicate it within the organization and then live it. Remember that when you do this, you should explain the process so people know how you came up with them. Then share the stories that were the basis of the value and the practices. If you put it all together, people will relate to it better."

"You may want to prepare a deck to make sure you communicate all the elements and do not miss any. You can then give it to your managers as well, so that the message is not lost as it goes through the organization."

"I believe this will help," said Ankit, "but it does not feel like it will be enough. I liked the part about building culture through shared stories. We need ways to make this more real to everyone and do it regularly."

"This is not really my area of expertise, but a colleague of mine, Anjali, has been an HR professional for more than 20 years and now guides companies on sustaining culture. I knew we were going to discuss this today, and asked her to join us after lunch," said Javed. "Maybe we can take a break at this time and reconvene after lunch."

"Thanks, Javed," said Ankit. "You are helping us beyond our expectations."

Anjali arrived a bit early and joined them for lunch. It turned out that Javed and Anjali had worked together in the past, and now often drew on the others' expertise as needed. During lunch, they went over the values they had come up with.

When they got back, Anjali said, "As I understand it, now that you have your values together, you want to build a sustainable culture. Let me make a couple of points. Every organization always has a culture. It may not be the one you want, and it may not be ingrained, but it will be there. Defining your values is a great start. There are two other things you could think about now. Communication and rituals.

Let us start with rituals. Do you have any?"

"I am not sure I understand exactly what you mean by rituals," said Subodh.

"Well, a ritual is a set of activities performed in a particular order. In an organization, there could be a bell to recognize achievement, a weekly huddle, an annual event—pretty much anything qualifies," said Anjali.

"Anytime a new employee joins, I send out an introductory email," said Ankit, "does that qualify?"

"Yes, it does," said Anjali. "Doing this signals to both the new employee and everyone else that each person is important in the company and warrants a mail. It is a good message, and one that is important to sustain. If you ever feel you should stop doing it, remember that you are sending the reverse message—that the company is getting bigger and each of you are no longer important to me. And it will be true, too."

"Wow, I never thought of it that way, but you are right. I am imagining how I would feel as an employee and this feels correct," said Kamini.

Over the next two hours, Anjali guided the group into deciding a set of rituals. She gave several ideas and emphasized that a few is better than many, because it is important to keep them going. They finally decided on three:

1. An annual picnic, with families. It would be just fun and an opportunity for everyone to get together with their families. It would be like a fair, with game stalls and fun food.
2. A monthly all-hands meeting at each location. This would be at the workplace, with a senior manager (in rotation) giving the highlights of the month, followed by recognizing examples of performance

and values, with a citation, and then a joint celebration of all the birthdays in the month with cake.
3. A weekly online seminar, every Thursday from 4pm to 5pm. Anyone wanting to take a session could write into HR and it would be reviewed by a peer group (selected by an organization wide voting process). Attendance will be optional.

"I like this set," said Kamini. "You have one ritual with families which is a great bonding method, another that brings your values to the forefront every month, and a third that promotes teamwork and learning."

Ankit nodded. "This was very useful Anjali, thanks."

Anjali smiled. "The other thing to focus on is Communication."

Kamini shrugged. "I think we all get that. Every management program speaks about its importance. Livewell has also been doing a lot of it. I get that it is important, but do we need more?"

Anjali was nodding as Kamini spoke. "You're right, both in that communication must be done and that Livewell seems to have enough channels. What I was hoping to discuss is the content of this communication."

"That's interesting," said Subodh. "You are saying that we should be looking at the quality of our messaging, not just the quantity and frequency."

"Precisely. For example, every quarter you have an online session for all employees where you present your results. I understand that it is a 45-minute session, followed by Q&A. Is that right?" asked Anjali.

"Yes, it is," said Ankit. "We all take a lot of effort to make the presentation and we have at least four people speak. We go over our financial performance as well as other metrics about how well we are doing and our plans using our OKRs."

"It's a great idea, ritual worthy," smiled Anjali. "You are ticking many boxes by preparing and having others speak as well. Your employees will feel you care about them enough to give them an update, some will like the facts and figures, and as long as you are presenting with confidence, they will feel that they company is in the right trajectory.

The question is, however, is this what you want to say or is this something that they would like to hear? I submit that the key to most communication is how you make people feel."

Ankit looked thoughtful. "During our initial bad times, I would talk to the team about what we were going through, our plans and why I thought we were going to be OK. I remember that making a big difference."

"Yes, that's perfect," said Anjali. "You were communicating Reality, Confidence and Hope. During bad times, that is what people need. And you were doing it often. Because people don't always understand things the first time, repetition is critical."

"And what do you do when times are good?" Kamini wanted to know.

"It changes to Trust, Confidence and Inspiration. Irrespective of good or bad times, candour about the current situation is always important. The only difference is that in good times people need to feel inspired to do more."

"I am already feeling inspired," said Subodh.

That was a good note to end the meeting with.

Annexure 1
Strategy Management Tools

There are many tools that help in the development of a robust strategy. I have been using management tools for more than three decades now. These tools help to structure your thinking. Many of these tools have been selected by me based on my personal choices, and you should select your own by deciding what works best for you.

I have organized these tools into four categories, but it is not a ranked list. These tools are all extensively covered in other books and articles. My website (www.ashishbasu.com) contains links to some of the better explanations of the tools and how they are to be used. There is only one exception to this, and that is the Strategy Matrix. The Strategy Matrix is a tool I have developed and refined over the past 20 years. It is covered extensively in this book.

There are four types of tools given here:

1. Tools to help you understand and specify your business: These tools are excellent for representing company strategy. You can use them before strategy planning to show the current state of your company. Once the planning is complete, you can use them to show the new strategy.
2. Tools to define your business strategy: These are tools that help you think through and define your strategy. They should be revisited every year, and are versatile enough to continue to be used year after year.
3. Special tools for specific circumstances and companies: Use these tools if you meet the criteria mentioned in the brief outlines. If your company is one where one of these tools work, it will be particularly useful.

4. Tools that help execute your strategy: Once your strategy is clear, it needs to be executed within the organization. The tools in this section support deployment and will help you execute your strategy once you have come up with it.

Tools to Help Understand and Specify Your Business

1. Swot

This is a classic tool. Even if you use no other tool, the simple matrix of Strengths, Weaknesses (both internal), Opportunities and Threats (both environmental) is used in every planning exercise. It will allow you entire team to contribute to the exercise and to discuss the company and its environment in a simple way. Over time, other tools have developed around it. The Internal Factor Evaluation (IFE) Matrix and External Factor Evaluation (EFE) Matrix allow you to add weights to each of the SWOT elements so you do not waste time on the minor ones. Do look up TOWS (the name is derived by reversing SWOT). TOWS allow you to take the analysis from SWOT into strategic decision-making.

2. Porter's 5 Forces

Michael Porter literally wrote the book on competitive strategy. The 5 forces assume that a company's profitability is based on a combination of five competitive forces: Can new competitors enter your market easily? Can your customers substitute your product with another similar product category? Can your suppliers dictate your pricing and approach? Are your customers able to dictate your pricing and approach? And finally, how strong is your competition? Porter's model is most useful for understanding the viability of an industry. I often use a 15-point scoring approach to rate your competitiveness within your industry. Any industry with a score of 9 or lower, needs to either change the dynamics of the industry or diversify to support growth.

3. Pestel

PESTEL is a way to study the external and regulatory environment. PESTEL stands for Political, Economic, Social, Technological, Environmental and Legal factors. Your industry will certainly be affected by the first four elements or PEST. You may want to add E and L if your industry is impacted by environmental and legal factors—for example, if you are a company producing chemicals with by-products that need to be disposed carefully. You many consider adding elements of PESTEL into the Opportunities and Threats in your SWOT rather than doing it separately.

4. McKinsey's Seven Degrees of Freedom

The Seven Degrees of Freedom for Growth effectively covers all the various opportunities for growth that can be examined, in increasing levels of risk, cost and difficulty, along with higher revenue potential. Other tools covered in this list are better at thinking through your growth approach, but the Seven Degrees of Freedom for Growth is excellent to represent your growth strategy. The seven degrees are as follows: 1. Selling existing products to existing customers. 2. Acquiring new customers in existing markets. 3. Creating new products and services. 4. Developing new value-delivery approaches. 5. Moving into new geographies. 6. Creating a new industry structure. 7. Opening new competitive arenas.

5. Business Model Canvas

Of the tools given here, you should first fill out your Business Model Canvas or at least make sure you have all the answers required to do so. This document contains all key strategic elements of your business. If you are not aware of some of the elements here, please find out what those are before attempting a strategy definition exercise. The business model has nine parts and requires you to state your customer segment, value proposition, key resources, cost structure, channels, revenue streams, key activities, customer relationships and key partners. It essentially defines your business in one page (possibly in small font). On completing your strategic planning process, this is the document you must update.

Tools to Help You Define Your Business Strategy

6. Mission and Vision

The Mission Statement defines the purpose of the company, or 'why' the company exists. In defining your strategy, your discussions around the Mission will help you define what the company will and will not do. Your Vision Statement takes this further by setting a long-term goal—'what' your company seeks to achieve. Your Vision serves to focus the energy of the company and direct strategy. Together, the two of them provide you with the initial framework for revisiting your existing strategy.

7. Porters Value Chain

Michael Porter postulated that for any company to be truly and sustain-ably competitive, it must define very precisely who their customer is and how their product or service will uniquely meet some specific needs of that customer. He called it the Value Proposition. Using this approach, you must define/tune your business processes so that they are aligned to your Value Proposition. The processes that create and deliver your product to the customer is called the Value Chain. By uniquely aligning the Value Proposition and Value Chain, your company can improve its profits and keep its competitive advantage.

8. The Ansoff Matrix

In 1957, an applied mathematician, Igor Ansoff, published a paper in which he described four approaches to growth. These approaches depend on whether you want to focus on new markets, new products, neither or both. In his 2x2 matrix, he describes four possibilities: market penetration, market development, product development and diversification. It is elegant in its simplicity and relevance. Depending on your company's competencies and ambitions, it is advisable to have one of the growth strategies as your primary one and to develop another one for future business. Diversification is the riskiest, and you should evaluate that only if your company has no options for future growth in the others.

9. Strategy Canvas

In *Blue Ocean Strategy*, W. Chan Kim and Renee Mauborgne use the framework of Strategy Canvas to find unexplored opportunities and create new markets—defined by them as blue oceans. You can use this to show value beyond anything that competitors offer, thus creating new markets. Since new value propositions are defined, you can sometimes invest less in some parts of the conventional market offering, thus increasing your profitability. Discovering and exploiting blue oceans can result in explosive growth.

10. The Flywheel

In the book *Good to Great*, Jim Collins and his team studied companies over a long period of time to decide what made some of them great. One of the tools they developed in this study was the Flywheel. The principle of the Flywheel is that there are usually one or two sets of activities that are causal, the first causing the second and so on, till the last affects the first—creating a wheel. Each turn of the flywheel pushes the company forward, and doing it repetitively builds capabilities that keep you ahead of competition. The key here is the focus—instead of trying to be great at everything, be great at moving the flywheel along.

Special Tools for Specific Circumstances

11. McKinsey 7S model

In their book *In Search of Excellence*, Roger Waterman and Tom Peters name seven elements that successful organizations must focus on. All these start with the letter 'S', hence 7S. Of the seven, there are three 'hard' elements: Structure, Strategy and Systems. They are considered hard because they can be affected directly by management decisions. The other four are soft and linked to culture but equally important: Shared Values, Skills, Staff and Style. These four have to do with the culture of the organization. You can use this to ensure balance within your organization. If one element is strong, it tends to pull the others up, and if another is weak, it tends to make the rest less effective. You may want to select the one or two weakest elements to focus on. You will find it more useful if you are a mature organization in a mature market.

12. BCG Matrix

Developed by the Boston Consulting Group, the BCG Matrix is a 2x2 matrix that is particularly useful in evaluating a portfolio of products. The two dimensions are market growth and the relative market share of your product. Where both are low, the product is a 'dog' and you should consider divesting it. Where the market share is high, but growth is low, it is a 'cow' and you should use such products to generate cash for the other businesses. Where the market share is low but growth is high, it is a 'question mark', and you should study it carefully and decide to invest or divest. Where both are high, it is a 'star', and you should provide the lion's share of resources and attention to it.

13. 3 Circle Analysis

The three circles are your company attributes, competitor attributes and customer needs. By overlapping the three circles like a Venn diagram, you get nine sections. These nine areas clearly show you similarities and differences between you and competitors, and which of you is better at meeting customer needs. Where the overlap is large, you are in a commodity market, and should focus on differentiating yourself. When the sections are distinct, you should define what to highlight to customers and which abilities to build to neutralize competition. This tool is most valuable for companies addressing consumers in a competitive market.

14. Design Thinking

Design Thinking is usually applied to the development of products but is a great construct to examine business issues as well. Its principles were first described by Nobel Laureate Herbert Simon, and it is a five-step process focused on solving your customer's problem. The stages are Empathize, Define, Ideate, Prototype and Test. When you use Design Thinking you should focus on quick prototyping and an iterative development process. You must also have a deep understanding of your customer. Your solutions will usually affect the product or service, but they can also impact your internal processes, partnerships, markets, or even new segments.

15. Core Competencies

Initially described by C K Prahalad and Gary Hamel, the core competency framework is based on the premise that resources and skills together differentiate organizations and make them more competitive. Using this approach, you will examine your processes and products to ensure that they are leveraging your core competencies. It is effectively a resource-based approach to corporate strategy. If you are good at doing something and its critical to your business, working with core competencies is the right approach. Your focus then should be to develop your core competence, till you are the best at it, and leverage it for your business.

Tools That Help Execute Your Strategy

16. The Balanced Scorecard

Developed by David Nolan and Robert Kaplan, the BSC started out as a measurement framework. The BSC suggests a system of measurement that starts with Financial measures followed by Customer measures, Process measure, and Learning and Growth measures. It requires you to look at all your business functions and clearly see how each measurement contributes to reaching your financial goals. Over time it has evolved into a comprehensive management framework and you can use it to define organization goals and drive measurement and results across the organization.

17. The Strategy Matrix

The Strategy Matrix maps the Breakthrough Programs that your company will undertake in the near term against annual goals. The Matrix shows the correlations between them and is used to select programs and ensure that there are enough programs that the company has prioritized for the year. It also shows the targets, dates, and responsibilities for your company. Details are available in other sections of this book.

18. Objectives and Key Results

Initially started by Andy Grove of Intel, OKR has become popular after its adoption by many of the major technology companies including Google and LinkedIn. You will need to support each objective with a few (around three) Key Results, which are measures with short-term targets. You can deploy OKRs across the organization from the corporate level to teams and individuals. You will need to set Key Results every quarter, and then set up most reviews around the progress of these Key Results. The system is transparent (usually online and visible across the company), and individuals are encouraged to set their own goals. It is a powerful system for a rapidly changing industry.

19. Policy Deployment (Hoshin Kanri)

Policy Deployment was popularized by the Japanese in the 1980s and adopted by many organizations including HP. The system involves a process called 'catchball' where goals move both down the organization, with each level catching the ball from the higher level and passing back ideas and changes. It is a very comprehensive system of goal setting, resulting in a company-wide and detailed statement of goals and actions. In this system, every person would know exactly what was required of them. It is useful in organizations in markets which are more stable and unchanging.

20. Management by Objectives (MBO)

Management by Objectives is a popular deployment method implemented on conclusion of the annual planning process. When using MBO each function in your company takes the goals set at your company level and sets objectives for themselves and their direct reports, and so on down the organization. Objectives are clearly measurable and are regularly measured in company-wide deployments. These are then used both in reviews and in individual performance appraisals. Implementation is easier than Policy Deployment, but not easy to change within the year. It is however very well aligned to company goals and measures.

Annexure 2
Evaluate Your Readiness To Scale

Answer the questions given here to quickly evaluate how well your company is positioned on the four levers to scale.

Once you have shaded the circles, enter the Score for each question based on the Scoring provided. Hence if you Disagree with a statement, the Score will be -1. Double the given score if the item has a Star next to the question number. Add the scores for a lever to get the lever score.

		Scoring:	Strongly Disagree (0)	Disagree (1)	Neutral (2)	Agree (3)	Strongly Agree (4)	Score
Strategic Direction	1	Most employees can state the essential parts of our Mission and Vision	○	○	○	○	○	
	2	We know our customers well and understand how our products meet their needs	○	○	○	○	○	
	3	Our customers invariably like our products and services better than those of our customers	○	○	○	○	○	
	4*	We have a clear and proven approach to scale our business	○	○	○	○	○	
Breakthrough Initiatives	5	Our goals support our desire to scale	○	○	○	○	○	
	6	Our senior managers know our focus areas to scale in the next few quarters	○	○	○	○	○	
	7*	We have defined initiatives to help us scale	○	○	○	○	○	
	8	We execute our initiatives well	○	○	○	○	○	
Management Process	9	Most employees understand how to contribute to the goals of the company	○	○	○	○	○	
	10	All employees and divisions have clear goals	○	○	○	○	○	
	11*	We regulary review progress against goals with a view of helping meet those goals	○	○	○	○	○	
	12	Employees contribute to their own goals	○	○	○	○	○	
Culture & Competency	13	There is a strong sense of shared values in the company	○	○	○	○	○	
	14*	Employees openly and honestly share feedback and ideas with management	○	○	○	○	○	
	15	Employees volunteer to help organize a company event even without personal gain	○	○	○	○	○	
	16	We ensure the continuous development of skills and knowledge among our employees	○	○	○	○	○	

To interpret the scores for each lever, use the following table:

Score Range	Interpretation
15-20 (Excellent)	Congratulations, you are doing well on the lever. You may want to tweak some areas, but overall you are in good shape
11-14 (Functional)	While you are engaging with this lever, it can be done better. Look at the questions where your score is the lowest, to decide what actions you need to take. If some of your levers are lower than this, address them first.
6-10 (Stressed)	This lever is holding back your ability to scale. You can start by implementing some of the tools provided in this book.
0-5 (Absent)	This lever is either broken or does not exist, and it must be built before you can scale effectively.

www.ingramcontent.com/pod-product-compliance
Lightning Source LLC
Chambersburg PA
CBHW020908180526
45163CB00007B/2669